76483

THE LIBRARY
ST. MARY'S COLLEGE OF MA
ST. MARY'S CITY, MARYLAND

The Romantic Tradition in American Literature

The Romantic Tradition in American Literature

Advisory Editor

HAROLD BLOOM
Professor of English, Yale University

POEMS OF THE WAR

BY

GEORGE H[ENRY] BOKER

ARNO PRESS

A NEW YORK TIMES COMPANY

New York • 1972

Reprint Edition 1972 by Arno Press Inc.

Reprinted from a copy in The North Carolina
State Library

The Romantic Tradition in American Literature
ISBN for complete set: 0-405-04620-0
See last pages of this volume for titles.

Manufactured in the United States of America

ఱఎఱఎఱఎఱఎఱఎఱఎఱఎఱఎఱ

Library of Congress Cataloging in Publication Data

Boker, George Henry, 1823-1890.
   Poems of the war.

   (The Romantic tradition in American literature)
   1. United States--History--Civil War--Poetry.
I. Title. II. Series.
PS1105.P6 1972   811'.3   72-4949
ISBN 0-405-04623-5

POEMS OF THE WAR

BY

GEORGE H. BOKER.

BOSTON:
TICKNOR AND FIELDS.
1864.

Entered according to Act of Congress, in the year 1864, by

GEORGE H. BOKER,

in the Clerk's Office of the District Court for the District of Massachusetts.

.

UNIVERSITY PRESS:
WELCH, BIGELOW, AND COMPANY,
CAMBRIDGE.

CONTENTS.

	PAGE
INVOCATION	7

POEMS OF THE WAR.

THE RIDE TO CAMP	13
UPON THE HILL BEFORE CENTREVILLE	30
ZAGONYI	48
ON BOARD THE CUMBERLAND	51
THE SWORD-BEARER	61
THE BALLAD OF NEW ORLEANS	66
THE VARUNA	80
THE CROSSING AT FREDERICKSBURG	82
HOOKER'S ACROSS !	88
ERIC, THE MINSTREL	90
THE BLACK REGIMENT	99
BEFORE VICKSBURG	104
THE BATTLE OF LOOKOUT MOUNTAIN	107
IN THE WILDERNESS	116
ODE TO AMERICA	120
OREMUS	129
AD POETAS	133
THE FLAG	136

DRAGOON'S SONG 138

LANCER'S SONG 140

CAVALRY SONG 142

MARCH ALONG 144

THE FREE FLAG 147

SONG FOR THE LOYAL NATIONAL LEAGUE . . . 150

A BATTLE HYMN 153

HYMN FOR THE FOURTH OF JULY, 1863 . . . 156

SONNETS.

 "BLOOD, BLOOD!" 160

 "OH! CRAVEN, CRAVEN!" 162

 "BRAVE COMRADE, ANSWER!" 164

 GRANT 166

DIRGE FOR A SOLDIER 168

MISCELLANEOUS POEMS.

PRINCE ADEB 173

ABON'S CHARITY 186

IDLENESS 191

WINTER WINDS 194

ELISHA KENT KANE 196

DIRGE 200

INVOCATION.

O COUNTRY, bleeding from the heart,
    If these poor songs can touch thy woe,
And draw thee but awhile apart
    From sorrow's bitter overflow,
        Then not in vain
        This feeble strain
About the common air shall blow.

As David stood by prostrate Saul,
    So wait I at thy sacred feet :
I reverently raise thy pall,
    To see thy mighty bosom beat.
        I would not wrong
        Thy grief with song ;
I would but utter what is meet.

Arise, O giant! Lo, the day
   Flows hither from the gates of light.
The dreams, that struck thee with dismay,
   Were shadows of distempered night.
       'T is just to mourn
       What thou hast borne;
   But yet the future has its right.

A glory, greater than the lot
   Foretold by prophets, is to be;
A fame without the odious blot
   Upon thy title to be free, —
       The jeer of foes,
       The woe of woes,
   God's curse and sorrow over thee.

Above the nations of the earth
   Erect thee, prouder than before!
Consider well the trial's worth,
   And let the passing tempest roar!

It spends its shock
Upon a rock :
Thou shalt outlive a thousand more.

Through tears and blood I saw a gleam,
　　Through all the battle-smoke it shone ;
A voice I heard that drowned the scream
　　Of widows and the orphans' moan :
　　　　An awful voice
　　　　That cried, " Rejoice ! "
A light outbreaking from God's throne.

1 *

POEMS OF THE WAR.

THE RIDE TO CAMP.

WHEN all the leaves were red or brown,
    Or golden as the summer sun,
And now and then came flickering down
Upon the grasses hoar and dun,
    Through which the first faint breath of frost
    Had as a scorching vapor run ;
I rode, in solemn fancies lost,
    To join my troop, whose low tents shone
    Far vanward to our camping host.
Thus as I slowly journeyed on,
    I was made suddenly aware
    That I no longer rode alone.

Whence came that strange, incongruous pair ?
    Whether to make their presence plain
    To mortal eyes, from earth or air
The essence of these spirits twain
    Had clad itself in human guise,
    As in a robe, is question vain.
I hardly dared to turn my eyes,
    So faint my heart beat ; and my blood,
    Checked and bewildered with surprise,
Within its aching channels stood,
    And all the soldier in my heart
    Scarce mustered common hardihood.
But as I paused, with lips apart,
    Strong shame, as with a sturdy arm,
    Shook me, and made my spirit start,
And all my stagnant life grew warm ;
    Till with my new-found courage wild,
    Out of my mouth there burst a storm
Of song, as if I thus beguiled
    My way with careless melody :
    Whereat the silent figures smiled.

Then from a haughty, asking eye
   I scanned the uninvited pair,
   And waited sternly for reply.
One shape was more than mortal fair;
   He seemed embodied out of light;
   The sunbeams rippled through his hair;
His cheeks were of the color bright
   That dyes young evening, and his eyes
   Glowed like twin planets, that to sight
Increase in lustre and in size,
   The more intent and long our gaze.
   Full on the future's pain and prize,
Half seen through hanging cloud and haze,
   His steady, far and yearning look
   Blazed forth beneath his crown of bays.
His radiant vesture, as it shook,
   Dripped with great drops of golden dew;
   And at each step his white steed took,
The sparks beneath his hoof-prints flew;
   As if a half-cooled lava flood
   He trod, each firm step breaking through.

This figure seemed so wholly good,
   That as a moth which reels in light,
   Unknown till then, nor understood,
My dazzled soul swam ; and I might
   Have swooned, and in that presence died,
   From the mere splendor of the sight,
Had not his lips, serene with pride
   And cold, cruel purpose, made me swerve
   From aught their fierce curl might deride.
A clarion of a single curve
   Hung at his side by slender bands ;
   And when he blew, with faintest nerve,
Life burst throughout those lonely lands ;
   Graves yawned to hear, Time stood aghast,
   The whole world rose and clapped its hands.
Then on the other shape I cast
   My eyes.   I know not how or why
   He held my spell-bound vision fast.
Instinctive terror bade me fly,
   But curious wonder checked my will.
   The mysteries of his awful eye,

So dull, so deep, so dark, so chill,
   And the calm pity of his brow
   And massive features hard and still,
Lovely but threatening, and the bow
   Of his sad neck, as if he told
   Earth's graves and sorrows as they grow,
Cast me in musings manifold
   Before his pale, unanswering face.
   A thousand winters might have rolled
Above his head.   I saw no trace
   Of youth or age, of time or change,
   Upon his fixed immortal grace.
A smell of new-turned mould, a strange,
   Dank, earthen odor from him blew,
   Cold as the icy winds that range
The moving hills which sailors view
   Floating around the Northern Pole,
   With horrors to the shivering crew.
His garments, black as minéd coal,
   Cast midnight shadows on his way ;
   And as his black steed softly stole,

Cat-like and stealthy, jocund day
    Died out before him, and the grass,
    Then sere and tawny, turned to gray.
The hardy flowers that will not pass
    For the shrewd autumn's chilling rain,
    Closed their bright eyelids, and, alas !
No summer opened them again.
    The strong trees shuddered at his touch,
    And shook their foliage to the plain.
A sheaf of darts was in his clutch ;
    And wheresoe'er he turned the head
    Of any dart, its power was such
That nature quailed with mortal dread,
    And crippling pain and foul disease
    For sorrowing leagues around him spread.
Whene'er he cast o'er lands and seas
    That fatal shaft, there rose a groan ;
    And borne along on every breeze
Came up the church-bell's solemn tone,
    And cries that swept o'er open graves,
    And equal sobs from cot and throne.

Against the winds she tasks and braves,
  The tall ship paused, the sailors sighed,
  And something white slid in the waves.
One lamentation, far and wide,
  Followed behind that flying dart.
  Things soulless and immortal died,
As if they filled the self-same part;
  The flower, the girl, the oak, the man,
  Made the same dust from pith or heart.
Then spoke I, calmly as one can
  Who with his purpose curbs his fear,
  And thus to both my question ran.
" What two are ye who cross me here,
  Upon these desolated lands,
  Whose open fields lie waste and drear
Beneath the tramplings of the bands
  Which two great armies send abroad,
  With swords and torches in their hands ? "
To which the bright one, as a god
  Who slowly speaks the words of fate,
  Towards his dark comrade gave a nod,

And answered : " I anticipate
  The thought that is your own reply.
  You know him ; or the fear and hate
Upon your pallid features lie.
  Therefore I need not call him Death :
  But answer, soldier, who am I ? "
Thereat, with all his gathered breath,
  He blew his clarion ; and there came,
  From life above and life beneath,
Pale forms of vapor and of flame,
  Dim likenesses of men who rose
  Above their fellows by a name.
There curved the Roman's eagle nose,
  The Greek's fair brows, the Persian's beard,
  The Punic plume, the Norman bows ;
There the Crusader's lance was reared ;
  And there, in formal coat and vest,
  Stood modern chiefs ; and one appeared,
Whose arms were folded on his breast,
  And his round forehead bowed in thought,
  Who shone supreme above the rest.

Again the bright one quickly caught
  His words up, as the martial line
  Before my eyes dissolved to naught:
" Soldier, these heroes all are mine ;
  And I am Glory ! "   As a tomb
  That groans on opening, " Say, were thine,"
Cried the dark figure.   " I consume
  Thee and thy splendors utterly.
  More names have faded in my gloom
Than chronicles or poesy
  Have kept alive for babbling earth
  To boast of in despite of me."
The other cried, in scornful mirth,
  " Of all that was or is thou curse,
  Thou dost o'errate thy frightful worth !
Between the cradle and the hearse,
  What one of mine has lived unknown,
  Whether through triumph or reverse ?
For them the regal jewels shone,
  For them the battled line was spread ;
  Victorious or overthrown,

My splendor on their path was shed.
   They lived their life, they ruled their day:
   I hold no commerce with the dead.
Mistake me not, and falsely say,
   ‘ Lo, this is slow, laborious Fame,
   Who cares for what has passed away : ’ —
My twin-born brother, meek and tame,
   Who troops along with crippled Time,
   And shrinks at every cry of shame,
And halts at every stain and crime ;
   While I, through tears and blood and guilt,
   Stride on, remorseless and sublime.
War with his offspring as thou wilt ;
   Lay thy cold lips against their cheek.
   The poison or the dagger-hilt
Is what my desperate children seek.
   Their dust is rubbish on the hills ;
   Beyond the grave they would not speak.
Shall man surround his days with ills,
   And live as if his only care
   Were how to die, while full life thrills

His bounding blood ?   To plan and dare,
  To use life is life's proper end :
  Let death come when it will, and where ! "
" You prattle on, as babes that spend
  Their morning half within the brink
  Of the bright heaven from which they wend ;
But what I am, you dare not think.
  Thick, brooding shadow round me lies ;
  You stare till terror makes you wink ;
I go not, though you shut your eyes.
  Unclose again the loathful lid,
  And lo, I sit beneath the skies,
As Sphinx beside the pyramid ! "
  So Death, with solemn rise and fall
  Of voice, his sombre mind undid.
He paused ; resuming : " I am all ;
  I am the refuge and the rest ;
  The heart aches not beneath my pall.
O soldier, thou art young, unpressed
  By snarling grief's increasing swarm ;
  While joy is dancing in thy breast,

Fly from the future's fated harm;
   Rush where the fronts of battle meet,
   And let me take thee on my arm!"
Said Glory, " Warrior, fear deceit
   Where Death gives counsel. Run thy race;
   Bring the world cringing to thy feet!
Surely no better time nor place
   Than this, where all the Nation calls
   For help; and weakness and disgrace
Lag in her tents and council-halls;
   And down on aching heart and brain
   Blow after blow unbroken falls.
Her strength flows out through every vein;
   Mere time consumes her to the core;
   Her stubborn pride becomes her bane.
In vain she names her children o'er;
   They fail her in her hour of need;
   She mourns at desperation's door.
Be thine the hand to do the deed,
   To seize the sword, to mount the throne,
   And wear the purple as thy meed!

No heart shall grudge it ; not a groan
    Shall shame thee.   Ponder what it were
    To save a land thus twice thy own ! "
Use gave a more familiar air
    To my companions ; and I spoke
    My heart out to the ethereal pair.
" When in her wrath the nation broke
    Her easy rest of love and peace,
    I was the latest who awoke.
I sighed at passion's mad increase.
    I strained the traitors to my heart
    I said, ' We vex them ; let us cease.'
I would not play the common part.
    Tamely I heard the Southerns' brag :
    I said, 'Their wrongs have made them smart.'
At length they struck our ancient flag, —
    Their flag as ours, the traitors damned ! —
    And braved it with their patchwork rag.
I rose when other men had calmed
    Their anger in the marching throng ;
    I rose, as might a corpse embalmed,

Who hears God's mandate, ' Right my wrong ! '
   I rose and set me to his deed,
   With his great Spirit fixed and strong.
I swear that when I drew this sword,
   And joined the ranks, and sought the strife,
   I drew it in thy name, O Lord !
I drew against my brother's life,
   Even as Abraham on his child
   Drew slowly forth his priestly knife.
No thought of selfish ends defiled
   The holy fire that burned in me ;
   No gnawing care was thus beguiled.
My children clustered at my knee ;
   Upon my braided soldier's coat
   My wife looked — ah, so wearily ! —
It made her tender blue eyes float.
   And when my wheeling rowels rang,
   Or on the floor my sabre smote,
The sound went through her like a pang.
   I saw this ; and the days to come
   Forewarned me with an iron clang,

That drowned the music of the drum,
   That made the rousing bugle faint,
   And yet I sternly left my home.
Haply to fall by noisome taint
   Of foul disease, without a deed
   To sound in rhyme, or shine in paint ;
But oh, at least, to drop a seed,
   Humble but faithful to the last,
   Sown by my Country in her need !
O Death, come to me, slow or fast ;
   I 'll do my duty while I may.
   Though sorrow burdens every blast,
And want and hardship on me lay
   Their bony gripes, my life is pledged,
   And to my country given away !
Nor feel I any hope, new-fledged,
   Arise, strong Glory, at thy voice.
   Our sword the people's will has edged,
Our rule stands on the people's choice.
   This land would mourn beneath a crown,
   Where born slaves only could rejoice.

How should the Nation keep it down ?
  What would a despot's fortunes be,
  After his days of strength had flown,
Amidst this people, proud and free,
  Whose history from such sources run ?
  The thought is its own mockery.
I pity the audacious one
  Who may ascend that thorny throne,
  And bide a single setting sun.
Day dies ; my shadow's length has grown ;
  The sun is sliding down the West.
  That trumpet in my camp was blown.
From yonder high and wooded crest
  I shall behold my squadron's camp,
  Prepared to sleep its guarded rest
In the low, misty, poisoned damp
  That wears the strength, and saps the heart,
  And drains the surgeon's watching lamp.
Hence, phantoms ! in God's peace depart !
  I was not fashioned for your will :
  I scorn thy trump, and brave thy dart ! "

They grinned defiance, lingering still.
  "I charge ye quit me, in His name
  Who bore his cross against the hill ! —
By Him who died a death of shame,
  That I might live, and ye might die, —
  By Christ the martyr ! " As a flame
Leaps sideways when the wind is high,
  The bright one bounded from my side,
  At that dread name, without reply.
And Death drew in his mantle wide,
  And shuddered, and grew ghastly pale,
  As if his dart had pricked his side.
There came a breath, a lonely wail,
  Out of the silence o'er the land ;
  Whether from souls of bliss or bale,
What mortal brain may understand ?
  Only I marked the phantoms went
  Closely together, hand in hand,
As if upon one errand bent.

UPON THE HILL BEFORE CENTREVILLE.

July 21, 1861.

I 'LL tell you what I heard that day :
    I heard the great guns far away,
Boom after boom.   Their sullen sound
Shook all the shuddering air around,
And shook, ah me ! my shrinking ear,
And downward shook the hanging tear
That, in despite of manhood's pride,
Rolled o'er my face a scalding tide.
And then I prayed.   O God ! I prayed
As never stricken saint, who laid
His hot cheek to the holy tomb
Of Jesus, in the midnight gloom.

" What saw I ? "   Little.   Clouds of dust;
Great files of men, with standards thrust
Against their course ; dense columns crowned
With billowing steel.   Then, bound on bound,
The long black lines of cannon poured
Behind the horses, streaked and gored
With sweaty speed.   Anon shot by,
Like a lone meteor of the sky,
A single horseman ; and he shone
His bright face on me, and was gone.
All these, with rolling drums, with cheers,
With songs familiar to my ears,
Passed under the far hanging cloud,
And vanished ; and my heart was proud !

For mile on mile the line of war
Extended ; and a steady roar,
As of some distant stormy sea,
On the south wind came up to me.
And high in air, and over all,

Grew, like a fog, that murky pall,
Beneath whose gloom of dusty smoke
The cannon flamed, the bomb-shell broke,
And the sharp rattling volley rang,
And shrapnel roared, and bullets sang,
And fierce-eyed men, with panting breath,
Toiled onward at the work of death.

But when the sun had passed his stand
At noon, behold! on every hand
The dark brown vapor backward bore,
And fainter came the dreadful roar
From the huge sea of striving men.
Thus spoke my rising spirit then :
" Take comfort from that dying sound,
Faint heart, the foe is giving ground ! "
And one, who taxed his horse's powers,
Flung at me, " Ho ! the day is ours ! "
And scoured along.   So swift his pace,
I took no memory of his face.

Then turned I once again to Heaven ;
All things appeared so just and even ;
So clearly from the highest Cause
Traced I the downward-working laws, —
Those moral springs made evident
In the grand, triumph-crowned event.
So half I shouted and half sang,
Like Jephtha's daughter, to the clang
Of my spread, cymbal-striking palms,
Some fragments of thanksgiving psalms.

Meanwhile a solemn stillness fell
Upon the land.   O'er hill and dell
Failed every sound.   My heart stood still,
Waiting before some coming ill.
The silence was more sad and dread,
Under that canopy of lead,
Than the wild tumult of the war
That raged a little while before.
All nature in the work of death

Paused for one last, despairing breath ;
And cowering to the earth, I drew
From her strong breast my strength anew.

When I arose, I wondering saw
Another dusty vapor draw,
From the far right, its sluggish way
Towards the main cloud, that frowning lay
Against the westward sloping sun ;
And all the war was re-begun,
Ere this fresh marvel of my sense
Caught from my mind significance.
And then — why ask me ?   Oh ! my God !
Would I had lain beneath the sod,
A patient clod, for many a day,
And from my bones and mouldering clay
The rank field-grass and flowers had sprung,
Ere the base sight, that struck and stung
My very soul, confronted me,
Shamed at my own humanity.

O happy dead, who early fell,
Ye have no wretched tale to tell
Of causeless fear and coward flight,
Of victory snatched beneath your sight,
Of martial strength and honor lost,
Of mere life bought at any cost,
Of the deep, lingering mark of shame
Forever scorched on brow and name,
That no new deeds, however bright,
Shall banish from men's loathful sight!
Ye perished in your conscious pride,
Ere this vile scandal opened wide
A wound that cannot close nor heal;
Ye perished steel to levelled steel,
Stern votaries of the god of war,
Filled with his godhead to the core!
Ye died to live; these lived to die
Beneath the scorn of every eye!
How eloquent your voices sound
From the low chambers under ground!

How clear each separate title burns
From your high-set and laurelled urns !
While these, who walk about the earth,
Are blushing at their very birth ;
And though they talk, and go and come,
Their moving lips are worse than dumb.
Ye sleep beneath the valley's dew,
And all the nation mourns fcr you.
So sleep, till God shall wake the lands !
For angels, armed with fiery brands,
Await to take you by the hands.

The right-hand vapor broader grew ;
It rose, and joined itself unto
The main cloud with a sudden dash.
Loud and more near the cannon's crash
Came towards me, and I heard a sound
As if all hell had broken bound, —
A cry of agony and fear.
Still the dark vapor rolled more near,

Till at my very feet it tost
The vanward fragments of our host.
Can man, Thy image, sink so low,
Thou who hast bent thy tinted bow
Across the storm and raging main, —
Whose laws both loosen and restrain
The powers of earth, — without whose will
No sparrow's little life is still ?
Was fear of hell, or want of faith,
Or the brute's common dread of death,
The passion that began a chase
Whose goal was ruin and disgrace ?
What tongue the fearful sight may tell ?
What horrid nightmare ever fell
Upon the restless sleep of crime,
What history of another time,
What dismal vision, darkly seen
By the stern-featured Florentine,
Can give a hint to dimly draw
The likeness of the scene I saw ?

I saw, yet saw not.   In that sea,
That chaos of humanity,
No more the eye could catch and keep
A single point, than on the deep
The eye may mark a single wave
Where hurrying myriads leap and rave.
Men of all arms and all costumes,
Bare-headed, decked with broken plumes ;
Soldiers and officers, and those
Who wore but civil-suited clothes ;
On foot or mounted, — some bestrode
Steeds severed from their harnessed load ;
Wild mobs of white-topped wagons, cars
Of wounded, red with bleeding scars ;
The whole grim panoply of war
Surged on me with a deafening roar !
All shades of fear, disfiguring man,
Glared through their faces' brazen tan.
Not one a moment paused, or stood
To see what enemy pursued.

With shrieks of fear, and yells of pain,
With every muscle on the strain,
Onward the struggling masses bore.
O, had the foemen lain before,
They 'd trampled them to dusty gore,
And swept their lines and batteries
As autumn sweeps the windy trees !
Here one cast forth his wounded friend,
And with his sword or musket end
Urged on the horses ; there one trod
Upon the likeness of his God
As if 't were dust ; a coward here
Grew valiant with his very fear,
And struck his weaker comrade prone,
And struggled to the front alone.
All had one purpose, one sole aim,
That mocked the decency of shame,
To fly, by any means to fly ;
They cared not how, they asked not why.

I found a voice.   My burning blood
Flamed up.   Upon a mound I stood ;
I could no more restrain my voice
Than could the prophet of God's choice.
" Back, howling fugitives," I cried,
" Back, on your wretched lives, and hide
Your shame beneath your native clay !
Or if the foe affrights you, slay
Your baser selves ; and, dying, leave
Your children's tearful cheeks to grieve,
Not quail and blush, when you shall come,
Alive, to their degraded home !
Your wives will look askance with scorn ;
Your boys, and infants yet unborn,
Will curse you to God's holy face !
Heaven holds no pardon in its grace
For cowards.   O, are such as ye
The guardians of our liberty ?
Back, if one trace of manhood still
May nerve your arm and brace your will !

You stain your country in the eyes
Of Europe and her monarchies!
The despots laugh, the peoples groan,
Man's cause is lost and overthrown!
I curse you, by the sacred blood
That freely poured its purple flood
Down Bunker's heights, on Monmouth's
        plain,
From Georgia to the rocks of Maine!
I curse you, by the patriot band
Whose bones are crumbling in the land!
By those who saved what these had won! —
In the high name of Washington!"

Then I remember little more.
As the tide's rising waves, that pour
Over some low and rounded rock,
The coming mass, with one great shock,
Flowed o'er the shelter of my mound,
And raised me helpless from the ground.

As the huge shouldering billows bear,
Half in the sea and half in air,
A swimmer on their foaming crest,
So the foul throng beneath me pressed,
Swept me along with curse and blow,
And flung me — where, I ne'er shall
  know.

When I awoke, a steady rain
Made rivulets across the plain ;
And it was dark, — O, very dark !
I was so stunned as scarce to mark
The ghostly figures of the trees,
Or hear the sobbing of the breeze
That flung the wet leaves to and fro.
Upon me lay a dismal woe,
A boundless, superhuman grief,
That drew no promise of relief
From any hope.   Then I arose,
As one who struggles up from blows

By unseen hands ; and as I stood
Alone, I thought that God was good,
To hide, in clouds and driving rain,
Our low world from the angel train
Whose souls filled heroes when the earth
Was worthy of their noble birth.
By that dull instinct of the mind
Which leads aright the helpless blind,
I struggled onward, till the dawn
Across the eastern clouds had drawn
A narrow line of watery gray ;
And full before my vision lay
The great dome's gaunt and naked bones,
Beneath whose crown the nation thrones
Her queenly person.   On I stole,
With hanging head and abject soul,
Across the high embattled ridge,
And o'er the arches of the bridge.
So freshly pricked my sharp disgrace,
I feared to meet the human face.

Skulking, as any woman might
Who 'd lost her virtue in the night,
And sees the dreadful glare of day
Prepared to light her homeward way,
Alone, heart-broken, shamed, undone,
I staggered into Washington !

Since then long sluggish days have passed,
And on the wings of every blast
Have come the distant nations' sneers
To tingle in our blushing ears.
In woe and ashes, as was meet,
We wore the penitential sheet.
But now I breathe a purer air,
And from the depths of my despair
Awaken to a cheering morn,
Just breaking through the night forlorn,
A morn of hopeful victory.
Awake, my countrymen, with me !
Redeem the honor which you lost,
With any blood, at any cost !

I ask not how the war began,
Nor how the quarrel branched and ran
To this dread height.   The wrong or right
Stands clear before God's faultless sight.
I only feel the shameful blow,
I only see the scornful foe,
And vengeance burns in every vein
To die, or wipe away the stain.
The war-wise hero of the West,
Wearing his glories as a crest
Of trophies gathered in your sight,
Is arming for the coming fight.
Full well his wisdom apprehends
The duty and its mighty ends ;
The great occasion of the hour,
That never lay in human power
Since over Yorktown's tented plain
The red cross fell, nor rose again.
My humble pledge of faith I lay,
Dear comrade of my school-boy day,

Before thee, in the nation's view;
And if thy prophet prove untrue,
And from our country's grasp be thrown
The sceptre and the starry crown,
And thou and all thy marshalled host
Be baffled, and in ruin lost, —
O, let me not outlive the blow
That seals my country's overthrow!
And, lest this woful end come true,
Men of the North, I turn to you.
Display your vaunted flag once more,
Southward your eager columns pour!
Sound trump and fife and rallying drum;
From every hill and valley come!
Old men, yield up your treasured gold;
Can liberty be priced and sold?
Fair matrons, maids, and tender brides,
Gird weapons to your lovers' sides;
And, though your hearts break at the deed,
Give them your blessing and God-speed;

Then point them to the field of fame,
With words like those of Sparta's dame !
And when the ranks are full and strong,
And the whole army moves along,
A vast result of care and skill,
Obedient to the master will ;
And your young hero draws the sword,
And gives the last commanding word
That hurls your strength upon the foe, —
O, let them need no second blow !
Strike, as your fathers struck of old,
Through summer's heat and winter's cold ;
Through pain, disaster, and defeat ;
Through marches tracked with bloody feet ;
Through every ill that could befall
The holy cause that bound them all !
Strike as they struck for liberty !
Strike as they struck to make you free !
Strike for the crown of victory !

ZAGONYI.

Springfield, October 25, 1861.

BOLD Captain of the Body-Guard,
    I 'll troll a stave to thee !
My voice is somewhat harsh and hard,
    And rough my minstrelsy.
I 've cheered until my throat is sore
For how Dupont at Beaufort bore ;
    Yet here 's a cheer for thee !

I hear thy jingling spurs and reins,
    Thy sabre at thy knee ;
The blood runs lighter through my veins,
    As I before me see

Thy hundred men with thrusts and blows
Ride down a thousand stubborn foes,
   The foremost led by thee.

With pistol snap and rifle crack —
   Mere *salvos* fired to honor thee —
Ye plunge, and stamp, and shoot, and hack
   The way your swords make free ;
Then back again, — the path is wide
This time, — ye gods ! it was a ride,
   The ride they took with thee !

No guardsman of the whole command
   Halts, quails, or turns to flee ;
With bloody spur and steady hand
   They gallop where they see
Thy daring plume stream out ahead
O'er flying, wounded, dying, dead ;
   They can but follow thee.

3   D

So, Captain of the Body-Guard,
　　I pledge a health to thee !
I hope to see thy shoulders starred,
　　My Paladin ; and we
Shall laugh at fortune in the fray,
Whene'er you lead your well-known way
　　To death or victory !

ON BOARD THE CUMBERLAND.

MARCH 8, 1862.

" STAND to your guns, men!" Morris cried.
    Small need to pass the word ;
Our men at quarters ranged themselves
    Before the drum was heard.

And then began the sailors' jests :
    " What thing is that, I say ? "
" A long-shore meeting-house adrift
    Is standing down the bay ! "

A frown came over Morris' face ;
    The strange, dark craft he knew ;
" That is the iron Merrimac,
    Manned by a rebel crew.

" So shot your guns, and point them straight ;
   Before this day goes by,
We 'll try of what her metal 's made."
   A cheer was our reply.

" Remember, boys, this flag of ours
   Has seldom left its place ;
And where it falls, the deck it strikes
   Is covered with disgrace.

" I ask but this ; or sink or swim,
   Or live or nobly die,
My last sight upon earth may be
   To see that ensign fly ! "

Meanwhile the shapeless iron mass
   Came moving o'er the wave,
As gloomy as a passing hearse,
   As silent as the grave.

Her ports were closed ; from stem to stern
    No sign of life appeared.
We wondered, questioned, strained our eyes,
    Joked, — everything but feared.

She reached our range. Our broadside rang,
    Our heavy pivots roared ;
And shot and shell, a fire of hell,
    Against her sides we poured.

God's mercy ! from her sloping roof
    The iron tempest glanced,
As hail bounds from a cottage thatch,
    And round her leaped and danced ;

Or when against her dusky hull
    We struck a fair, full blow,
The mighty, solid iron globes
    Were crumbled up like snow.

On, on, with fast increasing speed
  The silent monster came,
Though all our starboard battery
  Was one long line of flame.

She heeded not, no gun she fired,
  Straight on our bow she bore ;
Through riving plank and crashing frame
  Her furious way she tore.

Alas ! our beautiful, keen bow,
  That in the fiercest blast
So gently folded back the seas,
  They hardly felt we passed !

Alas ! alas ! my Cumberland,
  That ne'er knew grief before,
To be so gored, to feel so deep
  The tusk of that sea-boar !

Once more she backward drew a space,
　　Once more our side she rent ;
Then, in the wantonness of hate,
　　Her broadside through us sent.

The dead and dying round us lay,
　　But our foemen lay abeam ;
Her open port-holes maddened us ;
　　We fired with shout and scream.

We felt our vessel settling fast,
　　We knew our time was brief,
"Ho ! man the pumps!" But they who worked,
　　And fought not, wept with grief.

" O keep us but an hour afloat !
　　O, give us only time
To mete unto yon rebel crew
　　The measure of their crime ! "

From captain down to powder-boy
  No hand was idle then ;
Two soldiers, but by chance aboard,
  Fought on like sailor men.

And when a gun's crew lost a hand,
  Some bold marine stepped out,
And jerked his braided jacket off,
  And hauled the gun about.

Our forward magazine was drowned ;
  And up from the sick bay
Crawled out the wounded, red with blood,
  And round us gasping lay.

Yes, cheering, calling us by name,
  Struggling with failing breath
To keep their shipmates at the post
  Where glory strove with death.

With decks afloat, and powder gone,
   The last broadside we gave
From the guns' heated iron lips
   Burst out beneath the wave.

So sponges, rammers, and handspikes —
   As men-of-war's-men should —
We placed within their proper racks,
   And at our quarters stood.

" Up to the spar-deck ! save yourselves ! "
   Cried Selfridge. " Up, my men !
God grant that some of us may live
   To fight yon ship again ! "

We turned, — we did not like to go ;
   Yet staying seemed but vain,
Knee-deep in water ; so we left ;
   Some swore, some groaned with pain.

3*

We reached the deck.   There Randall stood :
   " Another turn, men, — so ! "
Calmly he aimed his pivot gun :
   " Now, Tenny, let her go ! "

It did our sore hearts good to hear
   The song our pivot sang,
As, rushing on from wave to wave,
   The whirring bomb-shell sprang.

Brave Randall leaped upon the gun,
   And waved his cap in sport ;
" Well done ! well aimed ! I saw that shell
   Go through an open port."

It was our last, our deadliest shot ;
   The deck was overflown ;
The poor ship staggered, lurched to port,
   And gave a living groan.

Down, down, as headlong through the waves
    Our gallant vessel rushed,
A thousand gurgling watery sounds
    Around my senses gushed.

Then I remember little more.
    One look to heaven I gave,
Where, like an angel's wing, I saw
    Our spotless ensign wave.

I tried to cheer.   I cannot say
    Whether I swam or sank ;
A blue mist closed around my eyes,
    And everything was blank.

When I awoke, a soldier lad,
    All dripping from the sea,
With two great tears upon his cheeks,
    Was bending over me.

I tried to speak.   He understood
　　The wish I could not speak.
He turned me.   There, thank God ! the flag
　　Still fluttered at the peak !

And there, while thread shall hang to thread,
　　O let that ensign fly !
The noblest constellation set
　　Against our northern sky.

A sign that we who live may claim
　　The peerage of the brave ;
A monument, that needs no scroll,
　　For those beneath the wave.

THE SWORD-BEARER.

MARCH 8, 1862.

BRAVE Morris saw the day was lost ;
    For nothing now remained,
On the wrecked and sinking Cumberland,
    But to save the flag unstained.

So he swore an oath in the sight of Heaven, —
    If he kept it the world can tell : —
" Before I strike to a rebel flag,
    I 'll sink to the gates of hell !

" Here, take my sword ; 't is in my way ;
    I shall trip o'er the useless steel ;
For I 'll meet the lot that falls to all
    With my shoulder at the wheel."

So the little negro took the sword ;
    And O with what reverent care,
Following his master step by step,
    He bore it here and there !

A thought had crept through his sluggish brain,
    And shone in his dusky face,
That somehow — he could not tell just how —
    'T was the sword of his trampled race.

And as Morris, great with his lion heart,
    Rushed onward, from gun to gun,
The little negro slid after him,
    Like a shadow in the sun.

But something of pomp and of curious pride
    The sable creature wore,
Which at any time but a time like that
    Would have made the ship's crew roar.

Over the wounded, dying, and dead,
   Like an usher of the rod,
The black page, full of his mighty trust,
   With dainty caution trod.

No heed he gave to the flying ball,
   No heed to the bursting shell ;
His duty was something more than life,
   And he strove to do it well.

Down, with our starry flag apeak,
   In the whirling sea we sank,
And captain and crew and the sword-bearer
   Were washed from the bloody plank.

They picked us up from the hungry waves ; —
   Alas ! not all ! — " And where,
Where is the faithful negro lad ? " —
   " Back oars ! avast ! look there ! "

We looked ; and, as Heaven may save my soul,
   I pledge you a sailor's word,
There, fathoms deep in the sea, he lay,
   Still grasping his master's sword !

We drew him out ; and many an hour
   We wrought with his rigid form,
Ere the almost smothered spark of life
   By slow degrees grew warm.

The first dull glance that his eyeballs rolled
   Was down towards his shrunken hand ;
And he smiled, and closed his eyes again
   As they fell on the rescued brand.

And no one touched the sacred sword,
   Till at length, when Morris came,
The little negro stretched it out,
   With his eager eyes aflame.

And if Morris wrung the poor boy's hand,
   And his words seemed hard to speak,
And tears ran down his manly cheeks,
   What tongue shall call him weak ?

B

THE BALLAD OF NEW ORLEANS.

April 24, 1862.

JUST as the hour was darkest,
 Just between night and day,
From the flag-ship shone the signal,
 " Get the squadrons under way."

Not a sound but the tramp of sailors,
 And the wheeling capstan's creak,
Arose from the busy vessels
 As the anchors came apeak.

The men worked on in silence,
 With never a shout or cheer,
Till 't was whispered from bow to quarter,
 " Start forward ! all is clear."

Then groaned the ponderous engine,
    Then floundered the whirling screw;
And as ship joined ship, the comrades
    Their lines of battle drew.

The moon through the fog was casting
    A blur of lurid light,
As the captain's latest order
    Was flashed into the night.

" Steam on ! and whatever fortune
    May follow the attack,
Sink with your bows all northward :
    No vessel must turn back ! "

'T was hard when we heard that order
    To smother a rising shout;
For it wakened the life within us,
    And we burned to give it out.

All wrapped in the foggy darkness,
   Brave Bailey moved ahead ;
And stem after stern, his gunboats
   To the starboard station led.

Next Farragut's stately flag-ship
   To port her head inclined ;
And midmost, and most in danger,
   Bell's squadron closed behind.

Ah ! many a prayer was murmured
   For the homes we ne'er might see ;
And the silence and night grew dreadful
   With the thought of what must be.

For many a tall, stout fellow
   Who stood at his quarters then,
In the damp and the dismal moonlight,
   Never saw the sun again.

Close down by the yellow river
  In their oozy graves they rot ;
Strange vines and strange weeds grow o'er them,
  And their far homes know them not.

But short was our time of musing ;
  For the rebel forts discerned
That the whole great fleet was moving,
  And their batteries on us turned.

Then Porter burst out from his mortars,
  In jets of fiery spray,
As if a volcano had opened
  Where his leaf-clad vessels lay.

Howling and screeching and whizzing
  The bomb-shells arched on high,
And then, like gigantic meteors,
  Dropped swiftly from the sky.

Dropped down on the low, doomed fortress
   A plague of iron death,
Shattering earth and granite to atoms
   With their puffs of sulphurous breath.

The whole air quaked and shuddered,
   As the huge globes rose and fell,
And the blazing shores looked awful
   As the open gates of hell.

Fort Jackson and Fort Saint Philip,
   And the battery on the right,
By this time were flashing and thundering
   Out into the murky night.

Through the hulks and the cables, sundered
   By the bold Itasca's crew,
Went Bailey in silence, though round him
   The shells and the grape-shot flew.

No answer he made to their welcome,
    Till abeam Saint Philip bore,
Then, O, but he sent them a greeting
    In his broadsides' steady roar !

Meanwhile, the old man, in the Hartford,
    Had ranged to Fort Jackson's side :
What a sight ! he slowed his engines
    Till he barely stemmed the tide ;

Yes, paused in that deadly tornado
    Of case-shot and shell and ball,
Not a cable's length from the fortress,
    And he lay there, wood to wall.

Have you any notion, you landsmen,
    Who have seen a field-fight won,
Of canister, grape-shot, and shrapnel
    Hurled out from a ten-inch gun ?

I tell you, the air is nigh solid
  With the howling iron flight ;
And 't was such a tempest blew o'er us
  Where the Hartford lay that night.

Perched aloft in the forward rigging,
  With his restless eyes aglow,
Sat Farragut, shouting his orders
  To the men who fought below.

And the fort's huge faces of granite
  Were splintered and rent in twain,
And the masses seemed slowly melting,
  Like snow in a torrid rain.

Now quicker and quicker we fired,
  Till between us and the foe
A torrent of blazing vapor
  Was leaping to and fro ;

While the fort, like a mighty caldron,
    Was boiling with flame and smoke,
And the stone flew aloft in fragments,
    And the brick into powder broke.

So thick fell the clouds o'er the river,
    You hardly could see your hand ;
When we heard, from the fore-mast rigging,
    Old Farragut's sharp command :

" Full head ! Steam across to Saint Philip !
    Starboard battery, mind your aim !
Forecastle there, shift your pivots !   Now,
    Give them a taste of the same ! "

Saint Philip grew faint in replying,
    Its voice of thunder was drowned ;
" But, ha ! what is this ?   Back the engines !
    Back, back, the ship is aground ! "

4

Straight down the swift current came sweeping
    A raft, spouting sparks and flame ;
Pushed on by an iron-clad rebel,
    Under our port-side it came.

At once the good Hartford was blazing,
    Below, aloft, fore and aft.
" We are lost ! "   " No, no ; we are moving ! "
    Away whirled the crackling raft.

The fire was soon quenched.   One last broadside
    We gave to the surly fort ;
For above us the rebel gunboats
    Were wheeling like devils at sport.

And into our vacant station
    Had glided a bulky form ;
'T was Craven's stout Brooklyn, demanding
    Her share of the furious storm.

We could hear the shot of Saint Philip
  Ring on her armor of chain,
And the crash of her answering broadside,
  Taking and giving again.

We could hear the low growl of Craven,
  And Lowry's voice clear and calm,
While they swept off the rebel ramparts
  As clean as your open palm.

Then ranging close under our quarter,
  Out burst from the smoky fogs
The queen of the waves, the Varuna,
  The ship of bold Charly Boggs.

He waved his blue cap as he passed us ;
  The blood of his glorious race,
Of Lawrence, the hero, was burning
  Once more in a living face.

Right and left flashed his heavy pieces,
  Rams, gunboats — it mattered not;
Wherever a rebel flag floated
  Was a target for his shot.

All burning and sinking around him
  Lay five of the foe ; but he,
The victor, seemed doomed with the vanquished,
  When along dashed gallant Lee.

And he took up the bloody conflict,
  And so well his part he bore,
That the river ran fire behind him,
  And glimmered from shore to shore.

But while powder would burn in a cannon,
  Till the water drowned his deck,
Boggs pounded away with his pivots
  From his slowly settling wreck.

I think our great captains in Heaven,
  As they looked upon those deeds,
Were proud of the flower of that navy,
  Of which they planted the seeds.

Paul Jones, the knight-errant of ocean,
  Decatur, the lord of the seas,
Hull, Lawrence, and Bainbridge, and Biddle,
  And Perry, the peer of all these!

If Porter beheld his descendant,
  With some human pride on his lip,
I trust, through the mercy of Heaven,
  His soul was forgiven that slip.

And thou, living veteran, Old Ironsides,
  The last of the splendid line,
Thou link 'twixt the old and new glory,
  I know what feelings were thine!

When the sun looked over the tree-tops,
  We found ourselves — Heaven knows how —
Above the grim forts ; and that instant
  A smoke broke from Farragut's bow.

And over the river came floating
  The sound of the morning gun ;
And the stars and stripes danced up the halyards,
  And glittered against the sun.

O, then what a shout from the squadrons !
  As flag followed flag, till the day
Was bright with the beautiful standard,
  And wild with the victors' huzza !

But three ships were missing.   The others
  Had passed through that current of flame ;
And each scar on their shattered bulwarks
  Was touched by the finger of Fame.

Below us, the forts of the rebels
    Lay in the trance of despair ;
Above us, uncovered and helpless,
    New Orleans clouded the air.

Again, in long lines we went steaming
    Away towards the city's smoke ;
And works were deserted before us,
    And columns of soldiers broke.

In vain the town clamored and struggled ;
    The flag at our peak ruled the hour ;
And under its shade, like a lion,
    Were resting the will and the power.

THE VARUNA.

SUNK APRIL 24, 1862.

WHO has not heard of the dauntless
    Varuna ?
Who has not heard of the deeds she has done ?
Who shall not hear, while the brown Mississippi
    Rushes along from the snow to the sun ?

Crippled and leaking she entered the battle,
    Sinking and burning she fought through the
        fray,
Crushed were her sides, and the waves ran
      across her,
    Ere, like a death-wounded lion at bay,
Sternly she closed in the last fatal grapple,
    Then in her triumph sank grandly away.

Five of the rebels, like satellites round her,
  Burned in her orbit of splendor and fear ;
One, like the Pleiad of mystical story,
  Shot, terror-stricken, beyond her dread sphere.

We who are waiting with crowns for the victors,
  Though we should offer the wealth of our
      store,
Load the Varuna from deck down to kelson,
  Still would be niggard, such tribute to pour
On courage so boundless. It beggars possession,
  It knocks for just payment at heaven's bright
      door.

Cherish the heroes who fought the Varuna ;
  Treat them as kings if they honor your way ;
Succor and comfort the sick and the wounded ;
  Oh ! for the dead, let us all kneel to pray !

4 *   F

THE CROSSING AT FREDER-
ICKSBURG.

DECEMBER 11, 1862.

I LAY in my tent at mid-day,
　　Too full of pain to die,
When I heard the voice of Burnside,
　　And an answering shout reply.

I heard the voice of the General, —
　　'T was firm, though low and sad ;
But the roar that followed his question
　　Laughed out till the hills were glad.

" O comrade, open the curtain,
　　And see where our men are bound,
For my heart is still in my bosom
　　At that terrible, mirthful sound.

" And hark what the General orders,
   For I could not catch his words ;
And what means that hurry and movement,
   That clash of muskets and swords ? "

" Lie still, lie still, my Captain,
   'T is a call for volunteers ;
And the noise that vexes your fever
   Is only our soldiers' cheers."

" Where go they ? " " Across the river."
   " O God ! and must I lie still,
While that drum and that measured trampling
   Move from me far down the hill ?

" How many ? " " I judge, four hundred."
   " Who are they ? I 'll know to a man."
" Our own Nineteenth and Twentieth,
   And the Seventh Michigan."

" O, to go, but to go with my comrades !
    Tear the curtain away from the hook ;
For I 'll see them march down to their glory,
    If I perish by the look ! "

They leaped in the rocking shallops.
    Ten offered where one could go ;
And the breeze was alive with laughter
    Till the boatmen began to row.

Then the shore, where the rebels harbored,
    Was fringed with a gush of flame,
And buzzing, like bees, o'er the water
    The swarms of their bullets came.

In silence, how dread and solemn !
    With courage, how grand and true !
Steadily, steadily onward
    The line of the shallops drew.

Not a whisper !   Each man was conscious
   He stood in the sight of death ;
So he bowed to the awful presence,
   And treasured his living breath.

'Twixt death in the air above them,
   And death in the waves below,
Through balls and grape and shrapnel
   They moved — my God, how slow !

And many a brave, stout fellow,
   Who sprang in the boats with mirth,
Ere they made that fatal crossing
   Was a load of lifeless earth.

And many a brave, stout fellow,
   Whose limbs with strength were rife,
Was torn and crushed and shattered, —
   A helpless wreck for life.

But yet the boats moved onward ;
   Through fire and lead they drove,
With the dark, still mass within them,
   And the floating stars above.

So loud and near it sounded,
   I started at the shout,
As the keels ground on the gravel,
   And the eager men burst out.

Cheer after cheer we sent them,
   As only armies can, —
Cheers for old Massachusetts,
   Cheers for young Michigan !

They formed in line of battle ;
   Not a man was out of place.
Then with levelled steel they hurled them
   Straight in the rebels' face.

" O, help me, help me, comrade !
 For tears my eyelids drown,
As I see their starry banners
 Stream up the smoking town.

" And see the noisy workmen
 O'er the lengthening bridges run,
And the troops that swarm to cross them
 When the rapid work be done.

" For the old heat, or a new one,
 Flames up in every vein ;
And with fever or with passion
 I am faint as death again.

" If this is death, I care not !
 Hear me, men, from rear to van ! —
One more cheer for Massachusetts,
 And one more for Michigan ! "

HOOKER'S ACROSS.

MAY 1, 1863.

HOOKER 's across ! Hooker 's across !
  Standards and guidons and lance-pen-
    nons toss
Over the land where he points with his blade,
Bristle the hill-top, and fill up the glade.
Who would not follow a leader whose blood
Has swelled, like our own, the battle's red
    flood ?
Who bore what we suffered, our wound and
    our pain, —
Bore them with patience, and dares them again ?
        Hooker 's across !

Hooker 's across ! Hooker 's across !
River of death, you shall make up our loss !
Out of your channel we summon each soul,
Over whose body your dark billows roll ;
Up from your borders we summon the dead,
From valleys and hills where they struggled
        and bled,
To joy in the vengeance the traitors shall feel
At the roar of our guns and the rush of our
        steel !
        Hooker 's across !

Hooker 's across ! Hooker 's across !
Fears to the wind, with our standards, we toss,
Moving together, straight on, with one breath,
Down to the outburst of passion and death.
O, in the depths of our spirits we know
If we fail now in the face of the foe,
Flee from the field with our flag soiled and dim,
We may return, but 't will not be with him !
        Hooker 's across !

ERIC, THE MINSTREL.

A PARABLE.

MAY 7, 1863.

IN a great ring the Danish barons sat;
　　Their bitter hearts were cold within their
　　　　breasts;
For all that day the fortunes of the fight
Had gone against them, and the Saxon axe
Had hewed their faces, driving them perforce
Back to their moated camp beside the sea.
So in the evening, one by one, they came,
Unsummoned, to the presence of the Prince
For further counsel; though no word as yet
Broke the dark circle, where they brooding sat
With their brown chins upon their sinewy
　　　　hands.

Much they bemoaned their lot with muffled
groans,
And hard, deep-chested spasms of wordless
pain ;
And many an eye rolled from the piléd arms
To the small harbor, where the rocking ships
Flashed their long spars against the setting sun,
And seemed to beckon them away. Of all
Ragner, the Prince, was gloomiest. His eyes
Were dull and filmy, as a slaughtered wolf's,
Turned up to wither in the staring moon.
His grizzly beard hung down across his knees,
So low he bent, and his great, open face
Was void and stagnant ; not a ray of thought
Glimmered upon it. Had not, now and then,
His thick breath hissed between his grinding
teeth,
Or a deep groan surged, like a breaking wave,
Through his whole form, none would have said
he lived.

He had staked all upon one fatal fight.
Loud had he boasted of his strength and skill,
His men, his weapons, and his discipline,
That bound them all together in one will.
Much had he sneered at other chiefs, whose
        deeds
Had failed before the foe, through lack of wit;
Vaunting himself, and stamping on their wrecks.
Was this the issue? — this sad, woe-begone,
Fear-stricken huddle of disheartened men?
His hopes had failed him.   A despiséd foe,
Famished, half-clad, unsandalled, scantly armed,
With torn and bleeding hands had struck his
        swords,
His cunning engines and far-flying shafts,
Down to this ruin: with them, too, the crown,
Growing in fancy o'er his princely house.
Ragner said naught; for there was naught to
        say,
That babbling gossips might not say as well,

Years hence, above the embers.　So he turned
His brow against the hide-walls of his tent,
And almost wept for shame.　The curtains
　　　shook :
A face as brilliant as the evening-star,
And cheerful as an angel's that has looked,
A moment since, upon the light of heaven,
Shone steadily above that darkened group,
And drew their eyes together towards its beams.
Eric, the minstrel, entered in the tent,
And softly stepped before the wretched chiefs,
With the bard's license.　"Ragner," he began,
" And you, pale comrades of his misery,
Is this a time for weakness ? this a time
To drop your manhood, and to change your
　　　sex,
Now while ye need a double share of strength,
Of skill and courage, to make good the loss
That fell upon you in to-day's mishap ?
Is this a time for gloomy brows, dead brains,

Slack hands and failing hearts ? Is this a time
To empty memory of its olden stores,
And turn your backs upon your history ?
Is this a time for sheep to nibble grass,
And fatten for the butcher, while the plain
Is red with corpses, only fit for wolves
And the swart ravens' talons ? If there was
Ever to Danish men the sudden need
Of all God's best endowments, it is now.
Rise, or your lives are forfeit for your sloth ! "
They bounded up, as if they felt the foe
Already hacking at their cowering backs,
And bent their glances towards the distant
       ships,
With sullen meaning. " Rise, rise higher yet !
And turn your faces frowning on the foe ;
Or you lose more than life, your honor, chiefs ;
The fame that made you, when yon sun arose,
All that you were." Then, with a feeble groan,
They all sank down upon the ground again.

Scorn flashed o'er Eric's features a hot light,
Like that which pulses in the summer nights,
Ruddy and frequent.   But he calmed himself;
And with a sigh, he took from off his arm
His Norman harp ; and whispered to himself,
In tones as tender as his mother used,
" This is the time to sing."   He wound his
   hands
Round the long wires, and every warbling string
Flickered before him, like a jet of flame
That leaps along the darkness.   And he sang
His nation's birth, its growing infancy,
Rocked on the billows in long, pointed ships.
And then he sang how tribe was joined to tribe
In the dark forests, falling with the growth
Of gathered people, till the teeming land
Waved yellow grain, and smoked with forges.
   How
The streams turned round upon the wheels in
   foam,

And ground and hammered slavishly for man.
Then he struck out in triumph from the cords,
And raised his voice, accordant to the theme,
The glory of his nation.   How she warred
With   neighboring   powers,   and   spread   her
          tongue and laws,
From the cramped borders where her strength
          was nursed,
Up towards the ice, and downward towards the
          sun.
The sea became her highway.   Here and there
She set her foot upon far distant shores,
And founded other nations.   On the name
The Norman carried to the Pyrenees,
He hung in rapture.   O'er and o'er again
He sang of Charlemagne and all his peers ;
Of Roncesvalles, and of Roland's horn,
Until the horn seemed peeling in their ears ;
Or sinking fainter with the hero's breath,
Lower and lower, till the dismal night

Sank down and settled upon Roland's corse.
Then he sang other fields, of happier fate ;
Drawing his pictures on the painted air
With harp and voice, as plainly to the sense
As any since have wrought with tinted brush ;
And snorting steeds and mail-clad men, in
    square,
In line, in column, thundered past their eyes ;
And banners waved, and lances splintered up
On ringing shields and hauberks ; till there
    came
The serious press, at arm's length, of the swords ;
When the foe paused, shook, wavered, turned,
    and fled,
With all the Norman barons, at his heels,
Shouting their triumph in the hot pursuit.
By this, the chiefs had started from the ground,
With the grand light of battle flaming out
From their red eyeballs ; and outside the tent,
A murmur circled from the listening host, —

A murmur ending in a shrill, wild cheer,
That made the blood fly leaping through the
      veins,
And sent the right hand seeking for the sword.
Then Ragner strode from out the tent, and saw
His hurrying soldiers buckling on their arms ;
And heard the tested bow-strings snap and
      twang,
And sheaves of arrows rattling as they swung ;
And all the sounds a forming army makes
Came up, like music, to his wondering ears.
So he drew forth his sword amidst his chiefs,
And their swords followed.   Then the minstrel
      stole,
Unthanked, away, to weep beside his harp,
Dejected, prayerful : but that field was won.

THE BLACK REGIMENT.

PORT HUDSON, MAY 27, 1863.

DARK as the clouds of even,
   Ranked in the western heaven,
Waiting the breath that lifts
All the dread mass, and drifts
Tempest and falling brand
Over a ruined land ; —
So still and orderly,
Arm to arm, knee to knee,
Waiting the great event,
Stands the black regiment.

Down the long dusky line
Teeth gleam and eyeballs shine ;

And the bright bayonet,
Bristling and firmly set,
Flashed with a purpose grand,
Long ere the sharp command
Of the fierce rolling drum
Told them their time had come,
Told them what work was sent
For the black regiment.

" Now," the flag-sergeant cried,
" Though death and hell betide,
Let the whole nation see
If we are fit to be
Free in this land ; or bound
Down, like the whining hound, —
Bound with red stripes of pain
In our old chains again ! "
O, what a shout there went
From the black regiment !

" Charge ! " Trump and drum awoke,
Onward the bondmen broke ;
Bayonet and sabre-stroke
Vainly opposed their rush.
Through the wild battle's crush,
With but one thought aflush,
Driving their lords like chaff,
In the guns' mouths they laugh ;
Or at the slippery brands
Leaping with open hands,
Down they tear man and horse,
Down in their awful course ;
Trampling with bloody heel
Over the crashing steel,
All their eyes forward bent,
Rushed the black regiment.

" Freedom ! " their battle-cry, —
" Freedom ! or leave to die ! "

Ah! and they meant the word,
Not as with us 'tis heard,
Not a mere party shout:
They gave their spirits out;
Trusted the end to God,
And on the gory sod
Rolled in triumphant blood.
Glad to strike one free blow,
Whether for weal or woe;
Glad to breathe one free breath,
Though on the lips of death.
Praying — alas! in vain! —
That they might fall again,
So they could once more see
That burst to liberty!
This was what " freedom " lent
To the black regiment.

Hundreds on hundreds fell;
But they are resting well;

Scourges and shackles strong
Never shall do them wrong.
O, to the living few,
Soldiers, be just and true !
Hail them as comrades tried ;
Fight with them side by side ;
Never, in field or tent,
Scorn the black regiment !

BEFORE VICKSBURG.

MAY 19, 1863.

WHILE Sherman stood beneath the hot-
test fire,
That from the lines of Vicksburg gleamed,
And bomb-shells tumbled in their smoky gyre,
And grape - shot hissed, and case - shot
screamed ;
Back from the front there came,
Weeping and sorely lame,
The merest child, the youngest face
Man ever saw in such a fearful place.

Stifling his tears, he limped his chief to meet ;
But when he paused, and tottering stood,

Around the circle of his little feet
    There spread a pool of bright, young blood.
        Shocked at his doleful case,
          Sherman cried, "Halt! front face!
    Who are you? Speak, my gallant boy!"
" A drummer, sir : — Fifty-fifth Illinois."

" Are you not hit?" "That 's nothing. Only
          send
    Some cartridges : our men are out ;
And the foe press us." " But, my little
          friend — "
    " Don't mind me ! Did you hear that shout?
        What if our men be driven ?
          O, for the love of Heaven,
    Send to my Colonel, General dear !"
" But you ?" " O, I shall easily find the rear."

" I 'll see to that," cried Sherman ; and a drop,
    Angels might envy, dimmed his eye,

        5 *

As the boy, toiling towards the hill's hard top,
   Turned round, and with his shrill child's cry
      Shouted, " O, don't forget !
      We 'll win the battle yet !
   But let our soldiers have some more,
More cartridges, sir, — calibre fifty-four ! "

THE BATTLE OF LOOKOUT MOUNTAIN.

NOVEMBER 24, 1863.

" GIVE me but two brigades," said Hooker,
    frowning at fortified Lookout ;
" And I 'll engage to sweep yon mountain clear
    of that mocking rebel rout."
At early morning came an order, that set the
    General's face aglow :
" Now," said he to his staff, " draw out my
    soldiers ! Grant says that I may go."

Hither and thither dashed each eager Colonel,
    to join his regiment,
While a low rumor of the daring purpose ran
    on from tent to tent.

For the long roll was sounding through the
    valley, and the keen trumpet's bray,
And the wild laughter of the swarthy veterans,
    who cried, " We fight to-day ! "

The solid tramp of infantry, the rumble of the
    great jolting gun,
The sharp, clear order, and the fierce steeds
    neighing, "Why's not the fight begun ? "
All these plain harbingers of sudden conflict
    broke on the startled ear ;
And last arose a sound that made your blood
    leap, the ringing battle-cheer.

The lower works were carried at one onset ;
    like a vast roaring sea
Of steel and fire, our soldiers from the trenches
    swept out the enemy ;

And we could see the gray-coats swarming up
    from the mountain's leafy base,
To join their comrades in the higher fastness,—
    for life or death the race !

Then our long line went winding up the moun-
    tain, in a huge serpent-track,
And the slant sun upon it flashed and glim-
    mered as on a dragon's back.
Higher and higher the column's head pushed
    onward, ere the rear moved a man ;
And soon the skirmish-lines their straggling
    volleys and single shots began.

Then the bald head of Lookout flamed and
    bellowed, and all its batteries woke,
And down the mountain poured the bomb-shells,
    puffing into our eyes their smoke ;

And balls and grape-shot rained upon our
    column, that bore the angry shower
As if it were no more than that soft dropping
    which scarcely stirs the flower.

O, glorious courage that inspires the hero, and
    runs through all his men !
The heart that failed beside the Rappahannock,
    it was itself again !
The star that circumstance and jealous faction
    shrouded in envious night
Here shone with all the splendor of its nature,
    and with a freer light !

Hark, hark ! there go the well-known crashing
    volleys, the long-continued roar
That swells and falls, but never ceases wholly
    until the fight is o'er.

Up towards the crystal gates of heaven ascend-
ing, the mortal tempest beat,
As if they sought to try their cause together
before God's very feet.

We saw our troops had gained a footing almost
beneath the topmost ledge,
And back and forth the rival lines went surging
upon the dizzy edge.
We saw, sometimes, our men fall backward
slowly, and groaned in our despair ;
Or cheered when now and then a stricken rebel
plunged out in open air,
Down, down, a thousand empty fathoms drop-
ping,— his God alone knows where !

At eve thick haze upon the mountain gathered,
with rising smoke stained black,
And not a glimpse of the contending armies
shone through the swirling rack.

Night fell o'er all ; but still they flashed their
    lightnings and rolled their thunders loud,
Though no man knew upon which side was
    going that battle in the cloud.

Night — what a night ! — of anxious thought
    and wonder, but still no tidings came
From the bare summit of the trembling moun-
    tain, still wrapped in mist and flame.
But towards the sleepless dawn, stillness, more
    dreadful than the fierce sound of war,
Settled o'er Nature, as if she stood breathless
    before the morning star.

As the sun rose, dense clouds of smoky vapor
    boiled from the valley's deeps,
Dragging their torn and ragged edges slowly
    up through the tree-clad steeps ;

And rose and rose, till Lookout, like a vision,
    above us grandly stood,
And over his bleak crags and storm-blanched
    headlands burst the warm golden flood.

Thousands of eyes were fixed upon the moun-
    tain, and thousands held their breath,
And the vast army, in the valley watching,
    seemed touched with sudden death.
High o'er us soared great Lookout, robed in
    purple, a glory on his face,
A human meaning in his hard, calm features,
    beneath that heavenly grace.

Out on a crag walked something — what? an
    eagle, that treads yon giddy height?
Surely no man! but still he clambered forward
    into the full, rich light.

H

Then up he started, with a sudden motion, and
    from the blazing crag
Flung to the morning breeze and sunny radi-
    ance the dear old starry flag!

Ah! then what followed?   Scarred and war-
    worn soldiers, like girls, flushed through
    their tan,
And down the thousand wrinkles of the battles
    a thousand tear-drops ran.
Men seized each other in returned embraces,
    and sobbed for very love;
A spirit, which made all that moment brothers,
    seemed falling from above.

And as we gazed, around the mountain's sum-
    mit our glittering files appeared,
Into the rebel works we saw them moving;
    and we — we cheered, we cheered!

And they above waved all their flags before us,
    and joined our frantic shout,
Standing, like demigods, in light and triumph
    upon their own Lookout!

IN THE WILDERNESS.

MAY 7, 1864.

[The incident contained in the following poem is narrated by a
correspondent of the New York Tribune in a letter from the
battle-field, dated " Wilderness, May 7, 1864."]

MANGLED, uncared for, suffering thro'
  the night
 With heavenly patience the poor boy had
   lain ;
Under the dreary shadows, left and right,
 Groaned on the wounded, stiffened out the
   slain.
  What faith sustained his lone,
  Brave heart to make no moan,
To send no cry from that blood-sprinkled sod,
Is a close mystery with him and God.

But when the light came, and the morning dew
   Glittered around him, like a golden lake,
And every dripping flower with deepened hue
   Looked through its tears for very pity's sake,
     He moved his aching head
     Upon his rugged bed,
And smiled as a blue violet, virgin-meek,
Laid her pure kiss upon his withered cheek.

At once there circled in his waking heart
   A thousand memories of distant home ;
Of how those same blue violets would start
   Along his native fields, and some would roam
     Down his dear humming brooks,
     To hide in secret nooks,
And, shyly met, in nodding circles swing,
Like gossips murmuring at belated Spring.

And then he thought of the belovéd hands
   That with his own had plucked the modest
     flower,

The blue-eyed maiden, crowned with golden
   bands,
 Who ruled as sovereign of that sunny hour.
  She at whose soft command
  He joined the mustering band,
She for whose sake he lay so firm and still,
Despite his pangs, nor questioned then her will.

So, lost in thought, scarce conscious of the deed,
 Culling the violets, here and there he crept
Slowly, — ah! slowly, — for his wound would
   bleed ;
 And the sweet flowers themselves half smiled,
  half wept,
  To be thus gathered in
  By hands so pale and thin,
By fingers trembling as they neatly laid
Stem upon stem, and bound them in a braid.

The strangest posy ever fashioned yet
 Was clasped against the bosom of the lad,

As we, the seekers for the wounded, set
   His form upon our shoulders bowed and sad;
      Though he but seemed to think
      How violets nod and wink ;
And as we cheered him, for the path was wild,
He only looked upon his flowers and smiled.

ODE TO AMERICA.

N O more of girls and wine,
　　No more of pastoral joys,
No after-sighing for some antique line
Of bearded kings, who, at their nation's birth,
　　As children play with toys,
Made merry with our earth :
　　No more, no more of these !
　　The girls are pale ;
　　The wine is drunken to the lees ;
Still are the bleatings of the woolly fold ;
The olden kings look thin and cold,
　　Like dim belated ghosts
　　That hurrying sail
Towards their dark graves,

Along the brightening coasts,
And sapphire hollows of the crested waves,
    Chased by the golden lances hurled
    From the young sun above his cloudy world.

    My country, let me turn to thee,
        With love and pride that glow
        Pure as twin altar-fires which blow
    Their flames together to one Deity.
            Look where I may,
            O land beneath the iron sway
        Of the strong hand ; —
O land gored through and through
        By thy own faithless brand ;
    Land of once happy homes,
            To whose now darkened doors
        The hand of sorrow comes,
            Early and late, and pours,
    With no soft prelude, or no warning beat,
    Her urn of bitter tears before thy feet !

6

O suffering, patient land,
   Thou bearest thy awful woe
So grandly, with such high command
   Of tears, that dare not flow
  For the great godlike smile
  Which crowns thy lips the while,
And stills thy mighty heart to move
As calmly on as when the hand of love
  Guided thy peaceful realm,
And idly swung the almost useless helm ;
  That I, who, in my erring thought,
   Have often wronged thy fame,
   By sneers and taunts of blame,
  Bow down with penitence o'erfraught,
   And pangs of reverent shame.

  Thy rulers put aside thy rights ;
   Thou murmurest not :
   They waste thy gold ;
Still thy great cause is not forgot.
Thy ancient foe grows loud, and bold

To proffer counsel, jeers, and spurns ;
    The swaggering coward burns
With new-found courage ; England smites
    Thy sensitive, proud cheek, —
Smites, like a craven, when she deems thee
      weak !
    Thy pale, stern features blush,
    Thy passionate arteries gush
    With hot rebellious blood :
But thou stillest the raging flood ;
Thou seemest to listen, in a patient hush,
    To the audacious kings,
    As they prattle empty things.
    Thy pale, stern features blush
From thy heart the churl is spurned ;
    But thy ready sinews pause,
    Remembering thy holy cause,
And the blow is not returned !

Not yet, not yet ! O, bear,
As the lion in his lair,

Whetting his teeth and gathering all his
      strength,
    Bears the insulting cry
    Of hunters drawing nigh
The dreadful door of his invaded home :
  Whence, with a roar and bound, at length —
    With bristling hair, with mane that rolls
      Above his fiery eyes,
    Like the tumultuous vapors of the skies,
Above the piercing lightning — he shall come,
    The lordly beast, whose lifted paw controls
      The fatal ends of life, and, in his wrath,
      Sweep from his onward path
The awe-struck phalanx of his enemies !
  I saw thy many squadrons file and form ;
  I saw them driving through a deadly storm
    Of shot and shell,
    Where thousands fell ;
    But who survived, ah ! they, indeed,
    Were soldiers true ; a race to breed

Avenging warriors, ripening for the day
When thou shalt cast thy shame away.
I saw thy mail-clad fleets, whose ponderous arms
    Laugh at the toys of Europe, daily grow
      By stream and silent lake.
      I saw them glide and take
The sheltered waters, as the wild swan glides,
With scarce a ripple at their moulded sides,
    To mar the current in its onward flow.
Swiftly they gathered, by the rising walls
      Of arméd ports ;
      Hither and thither at prodigious sports,
To try their watery wings, they sped ;
    Then snuffed a welcome from the briny
      breeze,
And, with one will, away they fled
    To join their dusky sisters of the seas !
      I saw it all ; and bending low,
        My lips against thy ear I set,
      With " Hist ! a hope begins to grow !
        Bear on, bear on ! Not yet, not yet ! "

O glory of our race,
Long suffering guardian of the free,
Thou who canst dare to be,
For a great purpose, in a lowly place ! —
Thou who canst stretch the olive o'er the wave,
And smite the master of the slave,
Yet wisely measure all
That might and must befall
Ere the great end shall crown the thing to be ! —
How shall I honor thee ?
How shall I fitly speak,
In song so faint and weak,
Of majesty and wisdom such as thine ?
For now the scales, so long
Held on the side of wrong,
To thee again incline ;
And thou mayst lift thy radiant head,
And bind thy ring of re-appearing stars
About thy forehead, and forget thy scars
In joy at holding that for which they bled !

Resume thy place, unchallenged now,
Nor bow thy glories to the haughtiest brow
    That wears a royal crown !
    False prophets scowled thee down,
And whispered darkly of thy coming fate :
    The cause, the way, the date,
They wrote for thee with the slow augur's
      hand. —
    Their lies were scrawled in sand !
    They perished utterly !
What is the splendor of the diadem,
The gilded throne, the broidered carpet-hem,
The purple robe, the sceptre, and the strain
    Of foregone kings, whose race
    Defies the herald's trace,
Before thy regal steps on land and main ?
    There are some deeds so grand
    That their mighty doers stand
Ennobled, in a moment, more than kings ;
    And such deeds, O land sublime,
    Need no sanctity from time ;

Their own epoch they create,

Whence all meaner things take date ;

Then exalt thee, for such noble deeds were
thine !

Envy nothing born of earth,

Rank nor wealth nor ancient birth,

Nor the glittering sorrows of a crown.

O Nation, take instead

Thy measureless renown,

To wrap thy young limbs like a royal stole,

And God's own flaming aureole,

To settle on thy head !

OREMUS.

WE will not raise, O God, the formal prayer
    Of broken heart and shattered nerve ;
Thou know'st our griefs, our wants, and what-
      soe'er
    Is best for those who serve.

Before Thy feet, in silence and in awe,
    We open lay our cause and need :
As brave men may, the patriot sword we draw,
    But Thine must be the deed.

We have no pageantry to please Thy eye,
    Save marshalled men, who marching come
Beneath Thy gaze in arméd panoply ;
    No music save the drum.

6 *
                  I

We have no altar, builded in Thy sight,
  From which the fragrant offerings rise,
Save this wide field of hot and bloody fight;
  These dead, our sacrifice.

To this great cause the force of prayer is given,
  The wordless prayer of righteous will;
Before whose strength the ivory gates of heaven
  Fall open, and are still.

For we believe, within our inmost souls,
  That what men do with spirit sad
To Thee in one vast cloud of worship rolls, —
  Rolls up, and makes Thee glad.

O God, if reason may presume so far,
  We say our cause is also Thine;
We read its truth in every flashing star,
  In every sacred line.

By Thy commission freedom first was sent,
    To hold the tyrant's force at bay ;
The chain that broke in Egypt, was not meant
    To bind our shining day.

Freedom to all ! in Thy great name we cry,
    And lift to heaven Thy bloody sword ;
Too long have we been blind in heart and eye
    To Thy outspoken word.

Before the terrors of that battle-call,
    As flax before the gusty flame,
Down, down, the vanquished enemy shall fall,
    Stricken with endless shame !

Here let division cease.   Join hand with hand,
    Join voice with voice ; a general shout
Shall, like a whirlwind, sweep our native land,
    And purge the traitors out !

Fear not or faint not.   God, who ruleth men,
   Marks where his noble martyrs lie :
They shall all rise beneath His smile again ;
   His foes alone shall die.

AD POETAS.

O BROTHER bards, why stand ye silent all,
  Amidst these days of noble strife,
While drum and fife and the fierce trumpet-call
  Awake the land to life ?

Now is the time, if ever time there was,
  To strike aloud the sounding lyre,
To touch the heroes of our holy cause
  Heart-deep with ancient fire.

'T is not for all, like Norman Taillefere,
  To sing before the warlike horde
Our fathers' glories, the great trust we bear,
  And strike with harp and sword.

Nor yet to frame a lay whose moving rhyme
    Shall flow in music North and South,
And fill with passion, till the end of time,
    The nation's choral mouth.

Yet surely, while our country rocks and reels,
    Your sweetly-warbled olden strains
Would mitigate the deadly shock she feels,
    And soothe her in her pains.

Some knight of old romance, in full career,
    Heard o'er his head the skylark sing,
And, pausing, leaned upon his bloody spear,
    Lost in that simple thing.

If by your songs no heroes shall be made
    To look death boldly eye to eye,
They may glide gently to the martyr's aid
    When he lies down to die.

And many a soldier, on his gory bed,
   May turn himself, with lessened pain,
And bless you for the tender words you said,
   Now singing in his brain.

So ye, who hold your breath amidst the fight,
   Be to your sacred calling true :
Sing on ! the far result is not in sight
   Of the great good ye do.

THE FLAG.

SEPTEMBER 22, 1862.

SPIRITS of patriots, hail in heaven again
   The flag for which ye fought and died,
Now that its field, washed clear of every stain,
   Floats out in honest pride !

Free blood flows through its scarlet veins once
      more,
   And brighter shine its silver bars ;
A deeper blue God's ether never wore
   Amongst the golden stars.

See how our earthly constellation gleams ;
   And backward, flash for flash, returns
Its heavenly sisters their immortal beams
   With light that fires and burns, —

That burns because a moving soul is there,
   A living force, a shaping will,
Whose law the fate-forecasting powers of air
   Acknowledge and fulfil.

At length the day, by prophets seen of old,
   Flames on the crimsoned battle-blade ;
Henceforth, O flag, no mortal bought and sold,
   Shall crouch beneath thy shade.

That shame has vanished in the darkened past,
   With all the wild chaotic wrongs
That held the struggling centuries shackled fast
   With fear's accursed thongs.

Therefore, O patriot fathers, in your eyes
   I brandish thus our banner pure :
Watch o'er us, bless us, from your peaceful skies,
   And make the issue sure !

DRAGOON'S SONG.

CLASH, clash goes the sabre against my
    steed's side,
Kling, kling go the rowels, as onward I ride ;
And all my bright harness is living and speaks,
And under my horseshoes the frosty ground
    creaks ;
I wave my buff glove to the girl whom I love,
Then join my dark squadron, and forward I
    move.

The foe, all secure, has lain down by his gun ;
I 'll open his eyelids before the bright sun.
I burst on his pickets ; they scatter, they fly ;
Too late they awaken, — 't is only to die.

Now the torch to their camp; I 'll make it a
      lamp,
As back to my quarters so slowly I tramp.

Kiss, kiss me, my darling! your lover is here.
Nay, kiss off the smoke-stains ; keep back that
        bright tear ;
Keep back that bright tear till the day when I
        come,
To the low wailing fife and deep muffled drum,
With a bullet half through this bosom so true,
To die, as I ought, for my country and you.

LANCER'S SONG.

A SIGH to the lips that we love from the
heart,
A scowl to the foe that is moving before us ;
Then mount, slacken reins, and spur hard for
the start,
With our pennons blown out, and our spears
slanted o'er us !

Who feels not his spirit mount up for this deed
Is a wretch, — in the soul of our souls we
abhor him ;
May he fall, like a dog, in the path of his steed,
And our close trampling hoofs in a torrent
sweep o'er him !

But who for his country shall fall on the field,
   O God, take his soul, if thou wilt not restore
      him ;
Make thy presence around him his comfort and
      shield,
   And gather thy angels, and spread their
      wings o'er him !

We have sighed our last sigh, we have prayed
      our last prayer :
   O country, the best of the life that's before us
We give thee ungrudging, in hope, not despair ;
   And we ask but thy tear when the volley
      rings o'er us.

CAVALRY SONG.

DRAW your girths tight, boys :
    This morning we ride,
With God and the right, boys,
   To sanction our side,
     Where the balls patter,
     Where the shot shatter,
     Where the shells scatter
Red death far and wide.

Pause not to think, boys,
   Of maidens in tears ;
Only this drink, boys,
   Let 's toss to our dears :

Then O for the battle,
The mad charging rattle,
The foam-snoi ting cattle,
The victors' wild cheers !

Look to your arms, boys,
  Your friends tried and true :
How the blood warms, boys !
  The foe is in view !
    Forward ! break cover !
    Ride through them ! ride over
    Them ! baptize the clover
With blood as with dew !

MARCH ALONG.

SOLDIERS are we from the mountain and
        valley,
  Soldiers are we from the hill and the plain ;
Under the flag of our fathers we rally ;
  Death, for its sake, is but living again.
      Then march along, gay and strong,
      March to battle with a song !
       March, march along !

We have a history told of our nation,
  We have a name that must never go down ;
Heroes achieved it through toil and privation ;
  Bear it on, bright with its ancient renown !
      Then march along, etc.

Who that shall dare say the flag waving o'er us,
   Which floated in glory from Texas to Maine,
Must fall, where our ancestors bore it before us,
   Writes his own fate on the roll of the slain.
     Then march along, etc.

Look at it, traitors, and blush to behold it !
   Quail as it flashes its stars in the sun !
Think you a hand in the nation will fold it,
   While there 's a hand that can level a gun ?
     Then march along, etc.

Carry it onward till victory earn it
   The rights it once owned in the land of the
      free ;
Then, in God's name, in our fury we 'll turn it
   Full on the treachery over the sea !
     Then march along, etc.

7   J

England shall feel what a vengeance the liar
   Stores in the bosom he aims to deceive ;
England shall feel how God's truth can inspire ;
   England shall feel it, but only to grieve.
      Then march along, etc.

Peace shall unite us again and forever,
   Though thousands lie cold in the graves of
      these wars ;
Those who survive them shall never prove,
      never,
   False to the flag of the stripes and the stars !
     Then march along, gay and strong,
     March to battle with a song !
      March, march along !

THE FREE FLAG.

JANUARY 1, 1863.

O HOLY ensign! symbol fair
  And unpolluted, save by those
 Whose crimes have made themselves thy foes,
Kiss with true love the taintless air!
Lay all thy starry clusters bare
  Beneath the heavenly stars; secure
  That, as their own, thy light is pure!

No more at thee the world shall sneer;
  No more beneath thy shade shall flash
  The terrors of the tyrant's lash;
Nor a whole race be bowed with fear,
As widens out thy grand career;

Nor shalt thou shield from righteous scorn
The guilt thy virtue has forsworn !

Where'er thy marshalled lines advance
　　The shattered chain shall fall behind ;
　　And in sad eyes, half blank, half blind,
The light of liberty shall dance ;
And the imbruted countenance
　　Shall warm with knowledge in the rays
　　That break on thy regenerate days !

Now thou hast purpose, strong and high,
　　Who doubts that right's assured success,
　　If not from man, from God, shall bless
Thy suffering fidelity
With more than mortal victory, —
　　With peace whose heart no more shall quake
　　Whene'er a loosened chain may shake ?

Fly on, fly on!   All hail to thee,
 Flag whose fair folds thy children's blood
 Has washed as in a running flood !
And may thy war-cry's burden be,
Alike to all, " Be free, be free ! "
 Perish the wretch who 'd see thee wave
 Again above the shrinking slave !

SONG

FOR THE LOYAL NATIONAL LEAGUE OF NEW YORK,
ON THE ANNIVERSARY OF THE ATTACK ON
FORT SUMTER,

APRIL 11, 1863.

WHEN our banner went down,
   With its ancient renown,
Betrayed and degraded by treason,
   Did they think, as it fell,
   What a passion would swell
Our hearts when we asked them the reason?
     O, then, rally, brave men,
     To the standard again,
   The flag that proclaims us a nation!
     We will fight, on its part,
     While there's life in a heart,
   And then trust to the next generation.

Although causeless the blow
That at Sumter laid low
That flag, it was seed for the morrow ;
   And a thousand flags flew,
   For the one that fell true,
As traitors have found to their sorrow.
     O, then, rally, brave men,
     To the standard again,
      The flag that proclaims us a nation !
      We will fight, on its part,
      While there 's life in a heart,
     And then trust to the next generation.

'T was in flashes of flame
It was brought to a shame
Till then unrecorded in story ;
   But in flashes as bright
   It shall rise in our sight,
And float over Sumter in glory !

O, then, rally, brave men,
To the standard again,
The flag that proclaims us a nation !
We will fight, on its part,
While there 's life in a heart,
And then trust to the next generation.

A BATTLE HYMN.

GOD, to Thee we humbly bow,
   With hand unarmed and naked brow ;
Musket, lance, and sheathed sword
At Thy feet we lay, O Lord !
Gone is all the soldier's boast
In the valor of the host ;
Kneeling here, we do our most.

Of ourselves we nothing know :
Thou, and Thou alone, canst show,
By the favor of Thy hand,
Who has drawn the guilty brand.

7 *

If our foemen have the right,
Show Thy judgment in our sight
Through the fortunes of the fight!

If our cause be pure and just,
Nerve our courage with Thy trust:
Scatter, in Thy bitter wrath,
All who cross the nation's path:
May the baffled traitors fly,
As the vapors from the sky
When Thy raging winds are high!

God of mercy, some must fall
In Thy holy cause.   Not all
Hope to sing the victor's lay,
When the sword is laid away.
Brief will be the prayers then said;
Falling at Thy altar dead,
Take the sacrifice instead!

Now, O God, once more we rise,
Marching on beneath Thy eyes ;
And we draw the sacred sword
In Thy name and at Thy word.
May our spirits clearly see
Thee, through all that is to be,
In defeat or victory !

HYMN

FOR THE FOURTH OF JULY, 1863.

L ORD, the people of the land
    In Thy presence humbly stand ;
On this day, when Thou didst free
Men of old from tyranny,
We, their children, bow to Thee.
    Help us, Lord, our only trust !
    We are helpless, we are dust !

All our homes are red with blood ;
Long our grief we have withstood ;
Every lintel, each door-post,

Drips, at tidings from the host,
With the blood of some one lost.
  Help us, Lord, our only trust !
  We are helpless, we are dust !

Comfort, Lord, the grieving one
Who bewails a stricken son !
Comfort, Lord, the weeping wife,
In her long, long widowed life,
Brooding o'er the fatal strife !
  Help us, Lord, our only trust !
  We are helpless, we are dust !

On our Nation's day of birth,
Bless Thy own long-favored earth !
Urge the soldier with Thy will !
Aid their leaders with Thy skill !
Let them hear Thy trumpet thrill !
  Help us, Lord, our only trust !
  We are helpless, we are dust !

Lord, we only fight for peace,
Fight that freedom may increase.
Give us back the peace of old,
When the land with plenty rolled,
And our banner awed the bold!
  Help us, Lord, our only trust!
  We are helpless, we are dust!

Lest we pray in thoughtless guilt,
Shape the future as Thou wilt!
Purge our realm from hoary crime
With Thy battles, dread, sublime,
In Thy well-appointed time!
  Help us, Lord, our only trust!
  We are helpless, we are dust!

With one heart the Nation's cries
From our choral lips arise:
Thou didst point a noble way
For our Fathers through the fray;

Lead their children thus to-day!
  Help us, Lord, our only trust!
  We are helpless, we are dust!

In His name, who bravely bore
Cross and crown begemmed with gore;
By His last immortal groan,
Ere He mounted to His throne,
Make our sacred cause Thy own!
  Help us, Lord, our only trust!
  We are helpless, we are dust!

B LOOD, blood ! The lines of every printed
        sheet
   Through their dark arteries reek with
      running gore ;
   At hearth, at board, before the household
      door,
   'T is the sole subject with which neighbors
      meet.
Girls at the feast, and children in the street,
   Prattle of horrors ; flash their little store
   Of simple jests against the cannon's roar,
   As if mere slaughter kept existence sweet.
O, heaven, I quail at the familiar way
   This fool, the world, disports his jingling
      cap ;
   Murdering or dying with one grin agap !

Our very Love comes draggled from the fray,
  Smiling at victory, scowling at mishap,
  With gory Death companioned and at
    play.

OH! craven, craven! while my brothers
    fall,
    Like grass before the mower, in the fight,
    I, easy vassal to my own delight,
    Am bound with flowers, a far too willing
        thrall.
Day after day along the streets I crawl,
    Shamed in my manhood, reddening at the
        sight
    Of every soldier who upholds the right
    With no more motive than his country's
        call.
I love thee more than honor; ay, above
    That simple duty, conscience-plain and
        clear
    To dullest minds, whose summons all men
        hear.

Yet as I blush and loiter, who should move
    In the grand marches, I cannot but fear
    That thou wilt scorn me for my very love.

BRAVE comrade, answer! When you
joined the war,
What left you? "Wife and children,
wealth and friends,
A storied home whose ancient roof-tree
bends
Above such thoughts as love tells o'er and
o'er."
Had you no pang or struggle? "Yes; I bore
Such pain on parting as at hell's gate rends
The entering soul, when from its grasp
ascends
The last faint virtue which on earth it
wore."
You loved your home, your kindred, children,
wife;

You loathed yet plunged into war's bloody
whirl! —
What urged you? "Duty! Something
more than life.
That which made Abraham bare the priestly
knife,
And Isaac kneel, or that young Hebrew
girl
Who sought her father coming from the
strife."

GRANT.

A S Moses stood upon the flaming hill,
    With all the people gathered at his feet,
    Waiting in Sinai's valley, there to meet
    The awful bearer of Jehovah's will ;
So, Grant, thou stand'st, amidst the trumpets
        shrill,
    And the wild fiery storms that flash and
        beat
    In iron thunder and in leaden sleet,
    Topmost of all, and most exposed to ill.
O, stand thou firm, great leader of our race,
    Hope of our future, till the times grow
        bland,
    And into ashes drops war's dying brand :

Then let us see thee, with benignant grace,
    Descend thy height, God's glory on thy
        face,
    And the law's tables safe within thy hand!

DIRGE FOR A SOLDIER.

IN MEMORY OF GENERAL PHILIP KEARNY.

KILLED SEPTEMBER 1, 1862.

CLOSE his eyes ; his work is done !
  What to him is friend or foeman,
Rise of moon, or set of sun,
  Hand of man, or kiss of woman ?
    Lay him low, lay him low,
    In the clover or the snow !
    What cares he ? he cannot know :
      Lay him low !

As man may, he fought his fight,
  Proved his truth by his endeavor ;

Let him sleep in solemn night,
  Sleep forever and forever.
    Lay him low, lay him low,
    In the clover or the snow !
    What cares he ? he cannot know :
      Lay him low !

Fold him in his country's stars,
  Roll the drum and fire the volley !
What to him are all our wars,
  What but death bemocking folly ?
    Lay him low, lay him low,
    In the clover or the snow !
    What cares he ? he cannot know :
      Lay him low !

Leave him to God's watching eye,
  Trust him to the hand that made him.
Mortal love weeps idly by :
  God alone has power to aid him.

8

Lay him low, lay him low,
In the clover or the snow !
What cares he ? he cannot know :
    Lay him low !

MISCELLANEOUS POEMS.

PRINCE ADEB.

IN Sana, O, in Sana, God, the Lord,
    Was very kind and merciful to me!
Forth from the Desert in my rags I came,
Weary and sore of foot.   I saw the spires
And swelling bubbles of the golden domes
Rise through the trees of Sana, and my heart
Grew great within me with the strength of God;
And I cried out, "Now shall I right myself, —
I, Adeb the despised, — for God is just!"
There he who wronged my father dwelt in
       peace, —
My warlike father, who, when gray hairs crept
Around his forehead, as on Lebanon
The whitening snows of winter, was betrayed
To the sly Imam, and his tented wealth

Swept from him, 'twixt the roosting of the cock
And his first crowing, — in a single night :
And I, poor Adeb, sole of all my race,
Smeared with my father's and my kinsmen's
        blood,
Fled through the Desert, till one day a tribe
Of hungry Bedouins found me in the sand,
Half mad with famine, and they took me up,
And made a slave of me, — of me, a prince !
All was fulfilled at last. I fled from them,
In rags and sorrow. Nothing but my heart,
Like a strong swimmer, bore me up against
The howling sea of my adversity.
At length o'er Sana, in the act to swoop,
I stood like a young eagle on a crag.
The traveller passed me with suspicious fear :
I asked for nothing ; I was not a thief.
The lean dogs snuffed around me : my lank
        bones,
Fed on the berries and the crusted pools,

Were a scant morsel.   Once, a brown-skinned
    girl
Called me a little from the common path,
And gave me figs and barley in a bag.
I paid her with a kiss, with nothing more,
And she looked glad ; for I was beautiful,
And virgin as a fountain, and as cold.
I stretched her bounty, pecking like a bird,
Her figs and barley, till my strength returned.
So when rich Sana lay beneath my eyes,
My foot was as the leopard's, and my hand
As heavy as the lion's brandished paw ;
And underneath my burnished skin the veins
And stretching muscles played, at every step,
In wondrous motion.   I was very strong.
I looked upon my body, as a bird
That bills his feathers ere he takes to flight, —
I, watching over Sana.   Then I prayed ;
And on a soft stone, wetted in the brook,
Ground my long knife ; and then I prayed
    again.

God heard my voice, preparing all for me,
As, softly stepping down the hills, I saw
The Imam's summer-palace all ablaze
In the last flash of sunset.   Every fount
Was spouting fire, and all the orange-trees
Bore blazing coals, and from the marble walls
And   gilded   spires   and   columns,   strangely
      wrought,
Glared the red light, until my eyes were pained
With the fierce splendor.   Till the night grew
      thick,
I lay within the bushes, next the door,
Still as a serpent, as invisible.
The   guard   hung   round   the   portal.   Man   by
      man
They dropped away, save one lone sentinel,
And on his eyes God's finger lightly fell;
He slept half standing.   Like a summer wind
That threads the grove, yet never turns a leaf,
I stole from shadow unto shadow forth;

Crossed all the marble court-yard, swung the
       door,
Like a soft gust, a little way ajar, —
My body's narrow width, no more, — and stood
Beneath the cresset in the painted hall.
I marvelled at the riches of my foe ;
I marvelled at God's ways with wicked men.
Then I reached forth, and took God's waiting
       hand :
And so He led me over mossy floors,
Flowered with the silken summer of Shiraz,
Straight to the Imam's chamber.   At the door
Stretched a brawn eunuch, blacker than my
       eyes :
His woolly head lay like the Kaba-stone
In Mecca's mosque, as silent and as huge.
I stepped across it, with my pointed knife
Just missing a full vein along his neck,
And, pushing by the curtains, there I was —
I, Adeb the despised — upon the spot

8 *   L

That, next to heaven, I longed for most of all.
I could have shouted for the joy in me.
Fierce pangs and flashes of bewildering light
Leaped through my brain and danced before
　　　my eyes.
So loud my heart beat, that I feared its sound
Would wake the sleeper; and the bubbling
　　　blood
Choked in my throat, till, weaker than a child,
I reeled against a column, and there hung
In a blind stupor.　Then I prayed again ;
And, sense by sense, I was made whole once
　　　more.
I touched myself; I was the same ; I knew
Myself to be lone Adeb, young and strong,
With nothing but a stride of empty air
Between me and God's justice.　In a sleep,
Thick with the fumes of the accursed grape,
Sprawled the false Imam.　On his shaggy
　　　breast,

Like a white lily heaving on the tide
Of some foul stream, the fairest woman slept
These roving eyes have ever looked upon.
Almost a child, her bosom barely showed
The change beyond her girlhood.　All her
　　　charms
Were budding, but half opened ; for I saw
Not only beauty wondrous in itself,
But possibility of more to be
In the full process of her blooming days.
I gazed upon her, and my heart grew soft,
As a parched pasture with the dew of heaven.
While thus I gazed she smiled, and slowly raised
The long curve of her lashes ; and we looked
Each upon each in wonder, not alarm, —
Not eye to eye, but soul to soul, we held
Each other for a moment.　All her life
Seemed centred in the circle of her eyes.
She stirred no limb ; her long-drawn, equal
　　　breath

Swelled out and ebbed away beneath her breast,
In calm unbroken.   Not a sign of fear
Touched the faint color on her oval cheek,
Or pinched the arches of her tender mouth.
She took me for a vision, and she lay
With her sleep's smile unaltered, as in doubt
Whether real life had stolen into her dreams,
Or dreaming stretched into her outer life.
I was not graceless to a woman's eyes.
The girls of Damar paused to see me pass,
I walking in my rags, yet beautiful.
One maiden said, " He has a prince's air ! "
I am a prince ; the air was all my own.
So thought the lily on the Imam's breast ;
And lightly as a summer mist, that lifts
Before the morning, so she floated up,
Without a sound or rustle of a robe,
From her coarse pillow, and before me stood
With asking eyes.   The Imam never moved.
A stride and blow were all my need, and they

Were wholly in my power. I took her hand,
I held a warning finger to my lips,
And whispered in her small, expectant ear,
" Adeb, the son of Akem ! " She replied
In a low murmur, whose bewildering sound
Almost lulled wakeful me to sleep, and sealed
The sleeper's lids in tenfold slumber, " Prince,
Lord of the Imam's life and of my heart,
Take all thou seest, — it is thy right, I know, —
But spare the Imam for thy own soul's sake ! "
Then I arrayed me in a robe of state,
Shining with gold and jewels ; and I bound
In my long turban gems that might have
           bought
The lands 'twixt Babelmandeb and Sahan.
I girt about me, with a blazing belt,
A scimitar o'er which the sweating smiths
In far Damascus hammered for long years,
Whose hilt and scabbard shot a trembling light
From diamonds and rubies. And she smiled,

As piece by piece I put the treasures on,
To see me look so fair, — in pride she smiled.
I hung long purses at my side.   I scooped,
From off a table, figs and dates and rice,
And bound them to my girdle in a sack.
Then over all I flung a snowy cloak,
And beckoned to the maiden.   So she stole
Forth like my shadow, past the sleeping wolf
Who wronged my father, o'er the woolly head
Of the swart eunuch, down the painted court,
And by the sentinel who standing slept.
Strongly against the portal, through my rags, —
My old base rags, — and through the maiden's
       veil,
I pressed my knife, — upon the wooden hilt
Was " Adeb, son of Akem," carved by me
In my long slavehood, — as a passing sign
To wait the Imam's waking.   Shadows cast
From two high-sailing clouds upon the sand
Passed not more noiseless than we two, as one,

Glided beneath the moonlight, till I smelt
The fragrance of the stables.   As I slid
The wide doors open, with a sudden bound
Uprose the startled horses ; but they stood
Still as the man who in a foreign land
Hears his strange language, when my Desert call,
As low and plaintive as the nested dove's,
Fell on their listening ears.   From stall to stall,
Feeling the horses with my groping hands,
I crept in darkness ; and at length I came
Upon two sister mares whose rounded sides,
Fine muzzles, and small heads, and pointed
          ears,
And foreheads spreading 'twixt their eyelids
          wide,
Long slender tails, thin manes, and coats of silk,
Told me, that, of the hundred steeds there
          stalled,
My hand was on the treasures.   O'er and o'er
I felt their bony joints, and down their legs

To the cool hoofs ; — no blemish anywhere :
These I led forth and saddled.   Upon one
I set the lily, gathered now for me, —
My own, henceforth, forever.   So we rode
Across the grass, beside the stony path,
Until we gained the highway that is lost,
Leading from Sana, in the eastern sands :
When, with a cry that both the Desert-born
Knew without hint from whip or goading spur,
We dashed into a gallop.   Far behind
In sparks and smoke the dusty highway rose ;
And ever on the maiden's face I saw,
When the moon flashed upon it, the strange
       smile
It wore on waking.   Once I kissed her mouth,
When she grew weary, and her strength re-
       turned.
All through the night we scoured between the
       hills :
The moon went down behind us, and the stars

Dropped after her ; but long before I saw
A planet blazing straight against our eyes,
The road had softened, and the shadowy hills
Had flattened out, and I could hear the hiss
Of sand spurned backward by the flying
        mares. —
Glory to God !   I was at home again !
The sun rose on us ; far and near I saw
The level Desert ; sky met sand all round.
We paused at mid-day by a palm-crowned well,
And ate and slumbered.   Somewhat, too, was
        said :
The words have slipped my memory.   That
        same eve
We rode sedately through a Hamoum camp, —
I, Adeb, prince amongst them, and my bride.
And ever since amongst them I have ridden,
A head and shoulders taller than the best ;
And ever since my days have been of gold,
My nights have been of silver, — God is just !

ABON'S CHARITY.

POOR, very poor had Abon Hassen grown ;
    Of all the wealth his fathers called their
        own
To him remained two sequins.   These he gave
To a low wretch, a miserable knave ;
As full of sin and falsehood as the brain
Of the big-eared and red-faced rogue, whose
        gain
Grew from long tables, heaped with bills and
        gold,
Beneath whose shade the loathsome beggar
        rolled,
And whined for alms, to every passer-by,
In Allah's name.   Young Abon's tender eye

Shone, like the morning sun, upon the place
Where lay the beggar ; and a regal grace
Crowned his fair forehead, as he quickly cast
His sequins down, and, blushing, onward passed,
With " Take them, then, in Allah's holy name :
Thy greater need, poor soul, puts mine to
       shame ! "
The youth passed quickly ; but the lying tongue
Of the vile wretch pursued, and round him rung
The old, stale blessings that for years had paid
Such simple victims, glib words of his trade ;
As bare of meaning, in their prayers and praise,
As to the parrot is the parrot's phrase.
But Abon paused, as if the seventh heaven
Before his eyes its ivory gates had riven ;
Paused with a strange, sweet warmth about his
       heart,
With music in his ears, and far apart
From this rough world one moment he was
       caught,

Beyond the bounds of sense or farthest thought,
Into the depths of an ecstatic trance ;
And there he reeled till rapture verged on pain.
Then slid he gently from that eminence ;
And Abon whispered, as he woke again,
" Surely the hand of Allah touched me then ! "

Out of the distance suddenly arose
A cry of terror ; then the rapid blows
Of flying hoofs, along the stony way,
Broke on his ears.   The crowd, in pale dismay,
Pressed back against the houses, leaving clear
The middle street ; down which, in mad career,
A furious horse, whose meteor mane and tail
Blew straight behind him, on the roaring gale
Of his own speed, rushed headlong.   And there
        clung
To the wild steed a form that toppling swung
Hither and thither in his giddy seat,
Helpless and failing.   An old man, more meet

For propping cushions on the soft divan,
Than that fierce throne, was he.   No venturous
       man,
Of all the throng, essayed to stop the course
Of the swift steed.   Now Abon knew a horse
As well as one may know his own right hand.
No breed or cross betwixt the sea and sand,
Syrian or Arab, but young Abon knew ;
And all their points of difference could view
In one quick glance.   So Abon, without heed
Or thought of danger, towards the maddened
      steed
Sprang, as the leopard bounds, and caught the
      bit.
Borne from his feet an instant, he alit
With his firm hand still on the golden shank
Of the long curb ; till on his haunches sank
The astonished horse, wide-eyed, subdued to
      naught.
Then from the saddle agile Abon caught

A mass of silks and jewels, falling prone
On his strong breast; and he who filled the
       throne
Of fair Damascus, without scratch or harm,
Lay safely panting upon Abon's arm.

When Abon Hassen, whom men call " the
       good,"
Years after, the Pasha, in counsel stood
With holy men before the mosque he raised
To hold his master's bones; and Osman praised
The glories of the temple; Abon told
The story of the beggar and the gold,
The trance, the flying horse; and how he
       stepped,
Watching the kingdom while his master slept,
Through actions spotless in the people's sight,
By slow advances to his princely height; —
Said Osman, holiest of the holy men,
" Surely the hand of Allah touched thee then !"

IDLENESS.

IF I do no more than this,
    I do something grand, I wis.
If I do no more than slumber
Where these locust-blossoms cumber
The young grass, while in and out
Voyage the humming bees about;
And the fields of new-turned land,
In long brown waves on every hand,
Mix their strong life-giving smell
With the violets of the dell,
Till I, half drunk with country gladness,
Forget the moody city-sadness; —

If I do no more than gaze,
Through the flimsy spring-tide haze,

Far into the sapphire deeps,
Where white cloud after white cloud creeps ;
Or watch the triumph of the sun,
When his western stand is won,
And crimson stain and golden bar
Are drawn across the evening-star ;
And slowly broaden on my sight
The glories of the deeper night,
Till I, o'ertaken with boding sorrow,
Shrink from inevitable to-morrow ; —

If I do no more than look
Into that dark and awful book
Which, like a prophet's fatal scroll,
Lies open in my deathless soul ;
Whose pictured joy and pictured woe
Mean more than any man may know ;
Close secret, hidden in death and birth,
Reflex and prophecy of earth ;

With earth's sweet sounds and scented blooms,
Its splendors and its solemn glooms,
All things the senses care about,
As clear within us as without ;
As if from us creation grew
In some strange way, we one time knew : —
If I do no more than this,
I do something grand, I wis.

WINTER WINDS.

O WINTER winds, your mournful roar
 Is burden of the song I sing;
An everlasting dirge ye pour,
A restless pain that beats the door
 Of heaven with its wounded wing.

Grief has no faith; the common woe
 That sees a future hope unfold,
Draws comfort thence; but as ye blow,
O winter winds, a grief I know
 That cannot, would not be consoled.

Ye wail o'er earth left desolate,
 O'er beauty stricken with decay;

Ye howl behind the path of fate,
Deaf to the voice that bids you wait,
  Ye cry for what has passed away.

And I who stand with drooping eyes,
  What heart have I to rise and greet
The beckoning hopes, that dimly rise,
While all I loved and trusted lies
  In ashes at my faltering feet ?

O winter winds, add moan to moan !
  For though ye give me no relief,
Ye sound a fitting undertone,
A dreary note whose heavy drone
  Keeps measure with my shriller grief.

ELISHA KENT KANE.

FEBRUARY 27, 1857.

O MOTHER Earth, thy task is done
 With him who slumbers here below;
From thy cold Arctic brow he won
 A glory purer than thy snow.

Thy warmer bosom gently nursed
 The dying hero; for his eye
The tropic Spring's full splendors burst, —
 " In vain ! " a thousand voices cry.

" In vain, in vain ! " The poet's art
 Forsook me when the people cried;
Naught but the grief that fills my heart,
 And memories of my friend, abide.

We parted in the midnight street,
  Beneath a cold autumnal rain ;
He wrung my hand, he stayed my feet
  With "Friend, we shall not meet again."

I laughed ; I would not then believe ;
  He smiled ; he left me ; all was o'er.
How much for my poor laugh I 'd give ! —
  How much to see him smile once more !

I know my lay bemeans the dead,
  That sorrow is an humble thing,
That I should sing his praise instead,
  And strike it on a higher string.

Let stronger minstrels raise their lay,
  And follow where his fame has flown ;
To the whole world belongs his praise,
  His friendship was to me alone.

So close against my heart he lay,
   That I should make his glory dim,
And hear a bashful whisper say,
   " I praise myself in praising him."

O gentle mother, following nigh
   His long, long funeral march, resign
To me the right to lift this cry,
   And part the sorrow that is thine.

O father, mourning by his bier,
   Forgive this song of little worth !
My eloquence is but a tear,
   I cannot, would not rise from earth.

O stricken brothers, broken band, —
   The link that held the jewel lost, —
I pray you give me leave to stand
   Amid you, from the sorrowing host.

We 'll give his honors to the world,
　　We 'll hark for echoes from afar ;
Where'er our country's flag 's unfurled
　　His name shall shine in every star.

We feel no fear that time shall keep
　　Our hero's memory.　Let us move
A little from the world to weep,
　　And for our portion take his love.

DIRGE.

A. W. November 20, 1863.

ANNIE'S dead, Annie 's dead!
In that sentence all is said.
Lily form and rosy head,
Still and cold, yet half divine;
Though the lights no longer shine
Whence her gentle soul looked through
Its clear essence, calmly true:
Ah! the solemn inward view
Those inverted eyeballs cast,
Ere her spirit heavenward passed!
              Annie 's dead!

   Annie 's dead, Annie 's dead!
Sister angels, overhead,
Have your greeting hands outspread;

Let a welcome cry be given,
As she treads the skirts of heaven ;
For a soul from earth more free,
More of your own purity,
Never joined your company.
Match her ye of heavenly mould,
Even thus, thus mortal cold !
        Annie 's dead !

   Annie 's dead, Annie 's dead !
Why should this be oversaid ?
Why should I abase my head ? —
I who loved her from afar,
As the dreamer may the star ;
I who bowed my humble eye,
Scarcely bold enough to sigh,
When she chanced to pass me by ;
Trembling lest a word might stir
The high calm that reigned in her.
        Annie 's dead !

Annie 's dead, Annie 's dead!
But a gleam of light hath sped
Through death's shadow close and dread ;
For wherever such as thou
Wanderest, must be sunshine now.
Dweller of some aery isle,
Floating up to God the while,
If I read aright that smile ;
Hear aright my heart that saith,
" Shall I fall in love with death ? "
          Annie 's dead !

THE END.

Cambridge : Stereotyped and Printed by Welch, Bigelow, & Co.

The Romantic Tradition in American Literature

An Arno Press Collection

Alcott, A. Bronson, editor. **Conversations with Children on the Gospels.** Boston, 1836/1837. Two volumes in one.

Bartol, C[yrus] A. **Discourses on the Christian Spirit and Life.** 2nd edition. Boston, 1850.

Boker, George H[enry]. **Poems of the War.** Boston, 1864.

Brooks, Charles T. **Poems, Original and Translated.** Selected and edited by W. P. Andrews. Boston, 1885.

Brownell, Henry Howard. **War-Lyrics** and Other Poems. Boston, 1866.

Brownson, O[restes] A. **Essays and Reviews Chiefly on Theology, Politics, and Socialism.** New York, 1852.

Channing, [William] Ellery (The Younger). **Poems.** Boston, 1843.

Channing, [William] Ellery (The Younger). **Poems of Sixty-Five Years.** Edited by F. B. Sanborn. Philadelphia and Concord, 1902.

Chivers, Thomas Holley. **Eonchs of Ruby:** A Gift of Love. New York, 1851.

Chivers, Thomas Holley. **Virginalia;** or, Songs of My Summer Nights. (Reprinted from *Research Classics,* No. 2, 1942). Philadelphia, 1853.

Cooke, Philip Pendleton. **Froissart Ballads,** and Other Poems. Philadelphia, 1847.

Cranch, Christopher Pearse. **The Bird and the Bell,** with Other Poems. Boston, 1875.

[Dall], Caroline W. Healey, editor. **Margaret and Her Friends.** Boston, 1895.

[D'Arusmont], Frances Wright. **A Few Days in Athens.** Boston, 1850.

Everett, Edward. **Orations and Speeches,** on Various Occasions. Boston, 1836.

Holland, J[osiah] G[ilbert]. **The Marble Prophecy,** and Other Poems. New York, 1872.

Huntington, William Reed. **Sonnets and a Dream.** Jamaica, N. Y., 1899.

Jackson, Helen [Hunt]. **Poems.** Boston, 1892.

Miller, Joaquin (Cincinnatus Hiner Miller). **The Complete Poetical Works of Joaquin Miller.** San Francisco, 1897.

Parker, Theodore. **A Discourse of Matters Pertaining to Religion.** Boston, 1842.

Pinkney, Edward C. **Poems.** Baltimore, 1838.

Reed, Sampson. **Observations on the Growth of the Mind.** *Including,* **Genius** (Reprinted from *Aesthetic Papers,* Boston, 1849). 5th edition. Boston, 1859.

Sill, Edward Rowland. **The Poetical Works of Edward Rowland Sill.** Boston and New York, 1906.

Simms, William Gilmore. **Poems:** Descriptive, Dramatic, Legendary and Contemplative. New York, 1853. Two volumes in one.

Simms, William Gilmore, editor. **War Poetry of the South.** New York, 1866.

Stickney, Trumbull. **The Poems of Trumbull Stickney.** Boston and New York, 1905.

Timrod, Henry. **The Poems of Henry Timrod.** Edited by Paul H. Hayne. New York, 1873.

Trowbridge, John Townsend. **The Poetical Works of John Townsend Trowbridge.** Boston and New York, 1903.

Very, Jones. **Essays and Poems.** [Edited by R. W. Emerson]. Boston, 1839.

Very, Jones. **Poems and Essays.** Boston and New York, 1886.

White, Richard Grant, editor. **Poetry:** Lyrical, Narrative, and Satirical of the Civil War. New York, 1866.

Wilde, Richard Henry. **Hesperia:** A Poem. Edited by His Son (William Wilde). Boston, 1867.

Willis, Nathaniel Parker. **The Poems, Sacred, Passionate, and Humorous, of Nathaniel Parker Willis.** New York, 1868.

A

THE LIBRARY
ST. MARY'S COLLEGE OF MARYLAND
ST. MARY'S CITY, MARYLAND 20686

76483